D0149287

OLIVES, ANCHOVIES, and CAPERS

OLIVES, ANCHOVIES, and CAPERS

the secret ingredients of the mediterranean table

by Georgeanne Brennan
Photographs by Leigh Beisch

CHRONICLE BOOKS
SAN FRANCISCO

Text copyright © 2001 by Georgeanne Brennan.
Photographs copyright © 2001 by Leigh Beisch.
All rights reserved. No part of this book may
be reproduced in any form without written
permission from the publisher.

Library of Congress Cataloging-in-Publication
Data available.
ISBN 0-8118-2494-2

Printed in Hong Kong.

Prop Stylist: Sara Slavin
Food Stylist: Sandra Cook
Photo Assistant: Sheri Giblin
Food Assistant: Jen McConnell
Designer: Sara Schneider

The photographer would like to thank Sara Slavin
and Sandra Cook for their remarkable creativity.

Distributed in Canada by Raincoast Books
9050 Shaughnessy Street
Vancouver, BC V6P 6E5

10 9 8 7 6 5 4 3 2 1

Chronicle Books LLC
85 Second Street
San Francisco, California 94105
www.chroniclebooks.com

TABLE OF CONTENTS

INTRODUCTION The Mediterranean region is one of the most beautiful places in the world—olive trees and vineyards, citrus groves and flowering herbs, oleander and bougainvillea, cloudless skies and an azure sea ringed with buildings in blazing white and lush pastels. A string of lazy days spent sitting in the sun or deep shade, sipping tea or wine, is the image that comes to mind. The Mediterranean also has some of the most delicious food in the world. It isn't complicated food, yet even the simplest dishes have a deep, fulfilling flavor that leaves you nearly breathless with satisfaction. A slice of garlic-rubbed toast spread with an unctuous olive paste or topped with a slice of fresh orange and an anchovy, a pile of crisply golden sardines and a lemon half, a grilled fish heaped with fresh tomatoes and capers, or a pilaf laced with zucchini and studded with black olives all deliver a sense of gustatory well-being out of proportion to the humble food. How can this be?

One reason is that from Tunisia and Morocco along the Mediterranean's southern shores, to the far eastern edges of Turkey and Syria, to the more familiar Mediterranean countries of Greece, Italy, France, and Spain, the traditional uses of three preserved ingredients, olives, anchovies, and capers, give the food an endless variation of character and depth.

Olives, anchovies, and capers are used not simply as garnishes, as we often think of them, but as integral additions to soups, salads, stews, sauces, spreads, and breads. These three cupboard staples are the secret ingredients of Mediterranean cooking, and learning to use them with a sure hand, both classically and creatively, broadens the cook's skill and saves time in the kitchen. One of the great virtues of using this indispensable trio is the amount and complexity of flavor that comes from the addition of a single ingredient, flavor that otherwise would only be achieved with many more ingredients and a reliance on time-consuming techniques such as reductions, larding, and infusions.

In my own kitchen, I have found that I readily use olives, anchovies, and capers in many preparations, relying upon them to balance the richness of a veal stew, to set off the sweetness of raisins or other dried fruits, and to interplay with tart-sweet flavors such as tomatoes, grapefruit, or fresh cheeses. It is easy to reach into the Mediterranean pantry and bring out a handful of olives to enhance braised greens, a few anchovies to add depth to a beef stew, or a sprinkling of capers to sharpen the flavor of a ragout of chicken and eggplant.

Fresh olives, capers, and anchovies are still preserved today–salted or packed in brine–in much the same manner they were during the time of the Phoenicians and the ancient Greeks and Romans. In the various countries bordering the Mediterranean, olives are prepared in dozens of different ways and may include the addition of herbs; spices; vegetables such as carrot, fennel, onion, and peppers; or the rinds of lemons and oranges. Anchovies are usually packed in coarse salt, although a few herbs might be added, or filleted, then packed in oil, either olive or another. They are also pickled in vinegar, sometimes along with herbs and peppercorns. Capers, the purists of the group, are cured in salt or vinegar, with other ingredients rarely added to the buds.

The preserving process itself, along with the added ingredients, produces complex flavors, and by using olives, anchovies, or capers (and sometimes all three) in a dish, Mediterranean cooks are able to achieve flavors that go far beyond what one expects from the addition of a single ingredient.

This doesn't mean that all the food tastes like this pungent pantry trio. On the contrary, when these ingredients are used as a seasoning, as they commonly are, it is frequently impossible to discern their taste in the dish at all. Instead, they bring out and enhance other flavors. Of course, when they are used as primary ingredients, their taste is in the forefront rather than the background.

In the following pages you will find short essays on olives, anchovies, and capers that address their attributes and explain how each is used in the Mediterranean style. Information on the cultivation and preservation of olives and capers and the fishing for and preservation of anchovies is included as well. The culinary differences among the various types of preserved anchovies are detailed, accompanied by guidelines on how to choose the best ones and instructions on how to salt your own anchovies and how to fillet whole ones. The different kinds of capers and olives are defined, so you may choose knowledgeably those that best suit your culinary needs. You'll also learn how to cure, brine, and season olives at home.

Along with the essays is a collection of recipes using olives, anchovies, and capers in a variety of different ways. Some of the preparations, such as Anchoïade, Salade Niçoise, Beef Ragout with Black Olives, and Baked Rockfish with Caper and Fennel Stuffing, are Mediterranean classics. Others, including Roast Chicken with Mustard-Anchovy Crust and Saffron Sea Bass Bowl, use the secret ingredients in inventive ways.

OLIVES The secret of using **olives** in cooking is to exploit not only the complexity of flavors that comes from the character of the individual **olive** variety itself, but also from the manner in which the **olive** was cured and seasoned. By adding a few **olives** to a salad, soup, stew, sauce, or a mound of bread dough, a palette of flavors is achieved that would normally require several different ingredients and techniques. Depending upon the type of **olive**, the taste of a particular dish can vary in multiple nuances. A tart Kalamata, for example, stirred into a chicken and tomato stew will slightly perk the acidity, but a salt-cured black **olive**, packed in **olive** oil, will contribute a mild, buttery character to the same stew. A spread made of green **olives** is quite different from one made with black **olives**, and an orange and anchovy salad with fennel-spiced green **olives** as a component will be a distant cousin of the same salad using black **olives** seasoned with peppers and garlic. The addition of a single ingredient, the **olive**, can direct the personality of the finished dish, a feature that makes a powerful pantry resident.

There is a wonderful variation in Mediterranean table **olives** and consequently a wide range of colors, sizes, and tastes. A display at any of the region's open markets will reveal not only **olives** that are green and black, but also purple, straw colored, burgundy, and brown. Some, like the Sevillano of Spain, are large and somewhat heart shaped, and others, like the Cailletiers of Nice, are as small as the tip of a little finger. Most of them are somewhere in between. They may be resting in brines flavored with fennel, lemon, orange peel, pepper, or bay leaves or other herbs, or they might be glistening with **olive** oil or salt. In addition to the substantial market selection presented by any respectable vendor, specialty **olives**, such as those pitted and stuffed with anchovies, almonds, or pimientos, are generally available.

The tremendous range of flavors among table **olives** is the result of several factors, including the variety itself, when and how they were picked, how they were cured, and if and how they have been further seasoned. Varieties differ from country to country. In Spain and Israel, the Manzanillo is one of the most common table **olives**, while in France it is more likely to be the picholine or Lucques, in Italy the Ascolano, in Greece the Kalamata, and in Tunisia the plump Meski. Of course, many others are used as well, but these are some of the **olives** destined for the table that are in the greatest production. Some table **olives**, like the Manzanillo and picholine, are picked green. The Kalamata, considered a black **olive**, is harvested when it is burgundy-black, and the Tanche, the buttery **olive** of Nyons, is picked fully black, when it is perfectly ripe but not yet wrinkled, as is the Gemlik, the most popular **olive** of Turkey.

The best table **olives** are taken from the trees by hand. Mechanical picking causes damage that diminishes their eating quality. In Tunisia, **olives** are harvested with plastic "claws," one on each of three fingers. Before plastic, the pickers outfitted themselves with hollowed-out goat horns. Using the claws, the **olives** are "raked" off the tree. In Italy and France, short, hand-held plastic rakes are employed. Either nets are cast beneath the trees to catch the **olives** as they fall, or if hand-picked, they are put one by one into baskets or buckets.

The curing process is begun as quickly as possible after picking, preferably within twenty-four hours. **Olives** must be cured before they can be eaten because fresh from the tree they contain a phenolic compound, oleuropein, which makes them bitter.

To remove or diminish the bitterness, **olives** are processed in a lye treatment, fermented in brine, packed in salt, or rinsed repeatedly in fresh water. **Olives** treated with lye or water are then packed in brine to preserve them. The brines vary in the herbs, spices, or other ingredients added to them, which accounts for some of the extensive flavor variation among these **olives**. Salt-cured **olives**, also called dry-cured or oil-cured **olives**, are packed in **olive** oil, with or without aromatics, after the cure is complete.

Both brine fermentation and salt packing also help to preserve the **olives**, although after the initial treatment they may be packed in fresh brine or salt, in **olive** oil or in vinegar, and sometimes with seasonings such as herbs, peppers, or citrus. Different regions and individual producers have their local specialties, of course, resulting in even more flavor variations.

Many Mediterranean families still make their own table **olives** using recipes handed down through generations. Each August when the **olives** turn from dusty apple green to shiny chartreuse, my neighbors in Haute Provence make *olives vertes cassées*. They gently crack open the meat of the **olive** with the back of a wooden spoon or a small mallet, then soak the **olives** in many rinses of water over many days before packing them in a fennel-flavored brine. These are the first **olives** of the season, wonderfully crisp and fresh tasting. They keep for only a month or so, but are the more valued because of their seasonality and short life span.

I know of families who live in Calabria, at the tip of Italy's boot, who traditionally pack burlap bags full of ripe black **olives** and soak them in seawater to cure them before packing them in brine. In other areas, **olives** that have been left to "sweeten" on the tree, that is, to shrivel until some of the bitterness leaves with the moisture, are considered highly desirable. Once picked, they are packed in jars just on their own, without brine, salt, or oil. They keep for years and may be brought out only for special guests. They are still quite bitter for most tastes, however, mine included.

An increasing number of imported **olives** are becoming readily available to us in the United States, giving the American consumer the opportunity to keep them in a Mediterranean-style pantry for quick flavoring. Experimenting with different kinds of **olives** will lead you to your own favorite choices.

In the recipes in this book I have typically indicated either brined green or black **olives** or salt-cured black **olives** (which are typically packed in oil) as general categories. Fermented **olives** such as the readily available Greek Kalamata, Spanish or Seville style, or Moroccan style may be used for brined **olives**. In almost every instance, you can change the selections, taking into consideration that the finished dish will reflect the character of the **olive** you choose.

As a rule, brine-cured **olives** should be rinsed before being used in cooking, as the clinging brine can add too much salt to a dish. There is no need to rinse salt-cured **olives**.

HOW TO CURE OLIVES

You can easily cure your own olives at home using the lye, water, or salt method. Fermenting olives in brine is more complicated and, due to bacterial formation, is best left to professionals. In all instances, begin with freshly picked, unblemished olives. Whether you pick the olives green or wait until they are black depends upon the method you are using.

lye curing

I was quite apprehensive about attempting this method until a friend walked me through the steps, and I have found that lye works well and quickly. Use 100 percent pure lye, and keep it far away from children. Select green olives, or those just beginning to show traces of burgundy, and place them in a nonreactive crock or vat, filling it no more than one-half to three-quarters full. In another nonreactive container, make a mixture of 4 ounces of lye for each 1 gallon of water. Stir to dissolve the lye. Pour the lye mixture over the olives, covering them completely. Place a clean towel on top of the olives, and weight them down with a plate topped with a brick. It is important to keep the olives submerged, because if exposed to the air, they will discolor and become mushy.

Every 12 hours, remove the weight, plate, and towel and, with a long-handled wooden or plastic spoon, reach down to the bottom and stir the olives, turning them from top to bottom. This is an important step, as it keeps the lye evenly distributed. Repeat for 4 or 5 days, or until the lye solution has penetrated nearly to the pit. Check the penetration daily by slicing an olive and observing the color change as the lye solution moves through the flesh. If the lye is allowed to penetrate only three-quarters of the way to the pit, the olives will retain a trace of their bitter fruit flavor, a desirable trait in much of the Mediterranean. Once the olives are done, drain and rinse them, then put them in fresh cold water for 6 to 12 hours to remove the lye. Repeat for a total of 5 changes of water.

Drain the olives a final time, place them in clean, dry jars, cover them with cooled brine (page 19), and tighten the lids. Store them in the refrigerator, where they will keep for up to 1 year. They are ready to eat after 1 week.

water curing

This method leaves more residual bitterness than the others, but for many Mediterraneans it is the bitter tang, the taste of the fruit itself, that is desirable. The bitterness is softened somewhat once the olives are brined. Choose olives that are green without the slightest hint of blush. Crack the meat with a mallet or the back of a wooden spoon, but don't break the pit. Put the olives in a nonreactive crock or vat and cover them with cold water. Change the water every day for at least 10 days or for up to 25 days, according to your taste. The longer the olives are in the water, the more bitterness they will lose, but they will always retain some. When you deem them to your taste, drain the water and put the olives in a clean, dry jar. Cover them with cooled brine (page 19) and tighten the lid. Store them in the refrigerator, where they will keep for up to 3 months. They are ready to eat after 1 week.

salt curing

The principle here, a method also referred to as oil curing, is to cover the olives, top and bottom, with a layer of salt. The salt draws out the moisture from the olives and with it the bitterness. People who salt-cure olives regularly have special curing boxes with holes drilled at the end for the runoff, but a variety of devices will work.

Choose very ripe, black olives; even slightly wrinkled ones are acceptable. If you wish to speed up the curing process, pierce them all over with pins that have been pushed through a slice of cork. Line a slatted wooden box with burlap, and cover the burlap with a 2-inch layer of rock salt. Add the olives and cover with more salt. Alternatively, make the layer of salt in the bottom of a burlap bag, add the olives, and cover them thoroughly with more salt. Place the box or bag above a bucket or sink to catch the liquid that will drain. Add more salt as it dissolves and drains away. The olives should be kept covered in salt until there is no longer any drainage. The bitterness will be leached in approximately 20 days, and the olives will not taste of salt, although they may be slightly wrinkled due to the moisture loss.

Once the olives are cured to your satisfaction, rinse and dry them. Put them in a clean, dry jar with a little fresh salt, dried thyme, and perhaps black peppercorns, dried red chiles, and bay leaves, and cover them with olive oil. Store them in the refrigerator, where they will keep for up to 1 year. They are ready to eat after 1 week. Since the oil congeals in the refrigerator, bring them to room temperature before serving.

Once the olives' bitterness has been removed with lye or water, a brine of water and salt, with or without additional flavoring, is used to store the olives. Unless you have a very cold cellar or similar location, however, the brined olives should be stored in the refrigerator. As a rule of thumb, figure on $1/2$ cup coarse sea salt or kosher salt for each 4 cups (1 quart) water. If the olives seem too salty for your taste after they have been in the brine, they may be soaked in fresh water for several hours or overnight to remove some of the salt. Keep tasting them until they are satisfactory.

BRINE makes 2 quarts

2 quarts water

1 cup coarse sea salt or kosher salt

3 fresh bay leaves, or 2 dried bay leaves

2 flowering fennel heads, or 1 tablespoon fennel seeds

3 or 4 fresh winter savory sprigs

3 or 4 fresh thyme sprigs

1 piece dried orange peel

1 tablespoon coriander seeds

1 tablespoon black peppercorns

In a saucepan, combine all the ingredients and bring to a boil over medium-high heat, stirring to dissolve the salt. Reduce the heat to medium and cook, uncovered, for 15 minutes. Remove from the heat and let cool completely before using.

ANCHOVIES

Since antiquity, **anchovies**, tiny, slim, silvery fish that swarm in schools in the Mediterranean Sea, have been considered an essential ingredient in the cooking of the region. Although fresh ones are eaten grilled, deep-fried, and even raw in quantity, especially in seaside towns, it is preserved **anchovies** that have made an indelible mark on Mediterranean cooking.

Whether simply sun-dried or packed in salt, oil, or vinegar, preserved **anchovies** share the near-magical ability to heighten the flavor and depth of a sauce, a spread, a soup, or a stew without displaying their own distinctive taste. For example, a few **anchovies** added to a slow-simmering beef-and-mushroom stew will increase the richness of the sauce, but you will detect not a trace of the anchovy flavor. In *tapenade*, the classic Provençal spread of olives, **anchovies**, and garlic pounded together, it is the olive that dominates, while the **anchovies** play the role of enhancer. In Sicilian green sauce made with lots of fresh herbs and used for fish, **anchovies** provide a depth of flavor and just a hint of the sea. **Anchovies** are often used in pastas and salads in conjunction with canned tuna, a particularly popular ingredient in Italy, Spain, and Tunisia. The **anchovies** help to bring out the flavor of the tuna without dominating the dish. On the other hand, *anchoïade*, another popular Provençal spread, is laden with intense anchovy flavor because the fish are the primary ingredient, pounded with only garlic and olive oil.

In yet another role, **anchovies**, which taste of both salt and the sea, furnish foods as diverse as fruits, greens, vegetables, grains, fowl, lamb, and beef with a complementary and complex flavor that some people, I among them, find irresistible. The sweet taste of oranges is accentuated by salty **anchovies**, but so is a chewy focaccia, a crisp pizza, or a pasta with tossed greens. A roasting chicken, well coated with a paste of mustard and **anchovies**, becomes robust and rich with the familiar taste of mustard attenuated with something stronger, deeper, and yet not quite discernible. Such is the magic of **anchovies**.

Depending upon the dish you are preparing you might want to choose between salt- or oil-packed **anchovies**, although they are essentially inter-changeable in terms of use, if not in texture. Salt-packed **anchovies**, which are whole fish, tend to have a firmer texture and a fresher flavor than their oil-packed counterparts. Oil-packed **anchovies** have been filleted, but they are sometimes soft and taste more of the oil in which they were packed than of the fish. This is not true of **anchovies** packed in good-quality olive oil. These are firm and meaty, and the olive oil supplies a positive note. In the recipes in this book where it makes a difference in the composition and final taste of the dish, I have indicated salt- or olive oil–packed **anchovies**; other-wise, I have simply indicated anchovy fillets. If you are using salt-packed **anchovies**, they will need to be filleted first, then rinsed (see page 24).

Much of the production of **anchovies** is still done the old-fashioned way. Collioure and Port-Vendres, both located in southwestern France near the Spanish border, have a long tradition of anchovy fishing and processing, as does Saint-Jean-de-Luz on the Atlantic Coast in the Basque country and Port Barbate near Gibraltar. The season is roughly from May to September or

October and the technique is basically the same from Italy and Greece to Spain, Morocco, and Tunisia. Small fishing boats go out at night and net the tiny fish, sometimes by lamplight, then come into the ports early in the morning to deliver the catch to the salting houses, where the fish are processed immediately by hand, a very labor-intensive process.

The innards and heads are removed, then the **anchovies** are first lightly processed in brine or directly packed in salt for a day or two, a step called presalting. The fish are lifted from this initial treatment, rinsed, and layered with salt in drums or barrels. Sometimes cinnabar (artificial red mercuric sulfide) is added to the salt, tinting the fish a reddish brown. Weights are laid on the packed barrels, to press out oil and moisture.

The fish are cured for up to a year, then removed from the salt and further processed by packing them whole in fresh salt or filleting them and packing them in oil. Usually the larger **anchovies**, those up to 5 inches long, are left whole. These are rinsed and dried before being repacked in layers of salt, some in retail-sized rounds, others in drums ranging from 1 kilo to 10 or even 20 kilos.

Anchovies to be packed in oil are first filleted by hand, and the tail, skin, and bones are removed. The fillets are packed side by side in rectangular tins, upright in glass jars, or in a star-shaped pattern in round tins; then an oil, usually from olives, but sometimes from soybeans or sunflowers, is added.

In the hot North African climate, **anchovies** are also dried. The fish are gutted and laid out to dry in the sun. The dried **anchovies** have an intense, yet pleasing flavor and a chewy texture.

Still other **anchovies**, notably in Spain, are processed in vinegar and aromatics and are known as white **anchovies**. These are typically served as a tapa or appetizer and are less commonly used in cooking.

FILLETING SALTED ANCHOVIES

Salt-packed anchovies must be filleted and rinsed before using, but it is a quick, easy process. First, rinse the salt from the fish under running cold water, then taste them. If they are too salty or too dry, soak them for 5 minutes in cold water. Milk can also be used for soaking, especially if the fish is particularly dry, as oversoaking in water will cause it to become soft and mushy and deteriorate.

Using your fingers or a sharp knife, lift the head and pull it and the backbone to which it is attached down toward the tail, leaving a fillet behind. Using your fingers or a knife, separate the remaining fillet from the bone, discarding the head and tail. If the fish is headless, simply pull downward on the bone. Remove any side fins. Depending on how you are using the anchovy, you may wish to remove the skin as well. To do so, gently rub the skin with your fingers under running water, and it will slip away.

SALTING FRESH ANCHOVIES

For centuries, people along the Mediterranean have been home-salting their own anchovies, and many early Mediterranean immigrants to the United States carried on that tradition, especially those who settled along the Pacific and Atlantic seaboards where fresh anchovies were available. It is a task easily accomplished in the home kitchen today, even by the novice. The key is to get very fresh anchovies from a knowledgeable fishmonger.

First, make a slit along the belly from just under the head to just before the tail, that is, from the gullet to the anus. Cut the head at the back and pull, removing the head and pulling out the innards. It may take a few tries to get the technique down, but once you learn it, you can dispense with the knife and use just your fingers. Rinse the cleaned fish and set aside. Continue until all the fish are cleaned. I do about 3 pounds at a time.

On a large tray or baking sheet or in a wooden box, make a 1-inch-thick layer of coarse sea salt. Top with a single layer of anchovies and cover with another layer of salt. Let stand for 3 to 4 hours or up to 24 hours. Remove the fish and pat them dry to remove the moisture that has been drawn out by the salt.

Next, in a glass jar or a ceramic crock with a lid, make a 1-inch-thick layer of coarse sea salt. (I use a widemouthed 2-quart canning jar.) Place a layer of fish on top of the salt, arranging them head to tail in concentric circles. Add a $^1\!/_2$-inch-thick layer of salt and repeat until all the anchovies have been used, ending with a layer of salt. Place a weight, such as a clean piece of brick or rock, on top of the final layer of salt and refrigerate for 2 to 3 days. Check at the end of the first day. The moisture drawn from the fish should be dissolving the salt into a coarse, slushy brine. If the salt does not dissolve, it will dehydrate the fish. To remedy the situation, dribble a teaspoon or two of water over the contents of the jar, put on the lid, and turn the jar once or twice. This is important, because the oil, which is being pressed from the fish, will go into the brine and rise to the surface. If the oil isn't removed, the fish will become rancid. At the end of the 2 or 3 days, carefully skim off the surface oil that has collected. Add more coarse sea salt as needed to cover and continue to store in a closed container in the refrigerator, using as desired. They will keep almost indefinitely, although it seems best to make a fresh batch yearly.

Anchovies can be found at the open markets, sold packed in salt or in oil, ready to be scooped up by the vendor and packed into a plastic bag or tub. Of course, you can also bring your own container to be filled. *Anchoïade*, a popular Provençal spread made of anchovies, capers, and olive oil, can be found ready-made from the vendors as well. Supermarkets, even modest ones, boast different styles of anchovies in sizes ranging from small jars and tins to over a pound, and they can also be found for sale in small grocery stores or small market stalls.

CAPERS The flower buds of the **caper** bush, *Capparis spinosa*, **capers** are a heat-loving, drought-tolerant shrub that thrives in the arid regions of the Mediterranean, including Morocco, Tunisia, Turkey, Spain, Israel, and Italy. Two of the Aeolian islands off the northern coast of Sicily, Pantelleria and Salina, are especially important sources for the pungent buds, and many Italians insist that the best **capers** come from these volcanic shards in the Tyrrhenian Sea.

Like anchovies and olives, **capers** are a processed product that, when used in cooking, contributes to a dish more depth of flavor than you would anticipate from any single ingredient. They are used in conjunction with fish, with tomatoes, and with anchovies and olives, and their flavor, which has been described as similar to mustard, imbues the dishes with a somewhat exotic heat. **Capers** are an important addition to salads, particularly ones composed of tuna, potatoes, bread, tomato, chicken, or variety meats where the distinctive flavor of the prized flower buds is an integral element. Scattered across the salad, the burnt olive-green spheres also provide an enticing appearance.

Capers add a piquancy to a wide variety of Mediterranean sauces. Most often they are puréed to make a thick paste, typically with ingredients such as garlic, parsley, almonds or walnuts, olives, anchovies, and, of course, olive oil. In France, *ravigote* sauce, a vinaigrette intensely flavored with **capers**, shallots, and herbs, is a companion to boiled meats such as tongue or head cheese, its tart flavor nicely balancing the richness of the meat. *Rémoulade*, another tart French sauce, is mayonnaise based and incorporates **capers** along with anchovies, pickles, and mustard. It is used primarily with fried fish, vegetables, and eggs. Sometimes a sauce is as simple as chopped **capers** mixed with melted butter and onion or bits of anchovy.

The buds sprout on low-lying, spreading bushes anywhere from $1\frac{1}{2}$ to 3 feet in diameter and about $1\frac{1}{2}$ feet tall. The plants grow wild in the cracks of stone walls and in the crevices of rocks–wherever they can find a foothold. The shrubs tend to drape and sprawl from their strongholds in the wild, but when cultivated they achieve a more orderly growth, aided by regular cultivation methods that improve the yield of the plant.

As a cultivated crop, **capers** are grown primarily in Spain and in Italy, although they are also cultivated, to a lesser extent, in France and Greece. Both cultivated and wild buds are hand-picked and undergo the same preserving processes. There are three types of preservation: in salt, in brine, and in vinegar. Regardless of the final packing, the **capers** are first layered with sea salt in barrels or vats. As the salt draws out the moisture, a brine forms that is stirred every day or so. After about 10 days, this first brine is poured off and fresh salt is added. A second brine forms and the **capers** are left in it for another 2 weeks or so before being drained, sized, and graded.

At this point, **capers** destined to be packed in salt are repacked with fresh salt and left undisturbed for about 2 months. They are then ready to eat but will keep for several years. This is the typical treatment in Italy. The Spanish style is to pack them in brine after the initial salting is completed. A third process involves fermentation followed by packing in vinegar, which is a popular French method, although salted ones are readily available, too.

If the **capers** are simply packed in salt, then rinsed before using, their full flavor remains most fully intact. **Capers** packed in brine or vinegar take on some of those flavors. They should be rinsed as well, to allow as much true **caper** flavor as possible to come to the fore.

In France, **capers** are sized and packed as Nonpareil extra fancy (5 to 6 mm), Nonpareil (7 mm), Surfine (8 mm), Capucine (9 mm), Capote (12 mm), and Hors Calibres (13 mm or greater). In Italy, they are graded on a scale of 7 to 16 millimeters. The flavor of **capers** is not determined by their size, however. Smaller ones are considered more valuable because they are less mature and thus firmer. They are also harder to pick because **capers** grow very quickly, so a small, perfect bud overlooked for a day or two quickly becomes a larger size. When size seems relevant, such as when making tiny, delicate appetizers or an elegant fish garnish, preference is given to smaller sizes. When **capers** are chopped, mashed, puréed, or otherwise incorporated into a dish, size doesn't really matter.

In the recipes in this book I have not indicated a preferred size, nor have I signaled using salted **capers** or those packed in vinegar or brine. Although the caveat stands that salt-packed **capers** have a fresher flavor, any **capers** may be used in the recipes with success. In every case, however, I advise you to rinse and drain them before using, thus the ingredient line asks for "**capers**, rinsed and drained."

CHAPTER 1: | APPETIZERS and SALADS

On the porch of a house overlooking the Mediterranean at Beaulieu-sur-Mer, a Provençal man served me this rustic combination with great flair and aplomb. He had called my friend and said if she would bring black olive bread from her noted village bakery, he would prepare an astonishing appetizer. She did and he did. It's the essence of simple, clean tastes. These are best prepared as you eat them, rather than ahead of time.

ANCHOVIES and LEMON on BLACK OLIVE BREAD   makes about 24; serves 8

1 loaf black olive bread or whole-wheat sturdy country bread
about $^1/_2$ cup unsalted butter, at room temperature
36 to 48 olive oil–packed anchovy fillets
3 or 4 lemons, halved

Cut the bread into slices a generous $^1/_4$ inch thick. Spread with a little butter, top with an anchovy fillet or two, and squeeze a little lemon juice on top. It's the lemon juice that does the trick. Serve at once.

Anchovies and eggs are frequently paired in France and Spain in composed salads or appetizers. Here, the yolks of hard-boiled eggs are mashed with anchovies to give a pleasantly pungent bite to old-fashioned stuffed eggs. For the perfect accompaniment, pour an aperitif of pastis, sherry, or a dry rosé.

ANCHOVY-STUFFED EGGS serves 4 to 6

6 hard-boiled eggs, peeled
6 anchovy fillets, minced
1 tablespoon Dijon mustard
2 teaspoons minced fresh flat-leaf parsley
$1/2$ teaspoon freshly ground black pepper

1 Cut the eggs in half lengthwise. Remove the yolks and put them in a bowl with the anchovies, mustard, 1 teaspoon of the parsley, and the pepper. Using the back of a fork, mash the ingredients together to make a rather stiff paste.

2 Slightly mound an equal amount of the mixture in the cavity of each egg half. Sprinkle with the remaining 1 teaspoon parsley to garnish. Serve at room temperature or chilled.

Sicilian cooks are known for their *caponata*, a sweet-sour relish made with eggplants, tomatoes, celery, capers, and green olives, but similar dishes are prepared elsewhere in the Mediterranean basin. This is a Provençal version, made with baked rather than fried eggplant, and the remaining ingredients are used raw rather than cooked. It can be served to accompany fish or meats, offered on its own as a salad, or set out with a collection of other little dishes for spreading on bread. If possible, use large, plump Sicilian capers (see Sources, page 126).

CAPONATA, PROVENÇAL STYLE
makes about 4 cups; serves 8

1 large eggplant

$1/4$ cup extra-virgin olive oil

4 or 5 tomatoes, peeled, seeded, and diced

1 small yellow onion, minced

1 to 2 cloves garlic, minced

$1/4$ cup capers, rinsed and drained

$1/2$ cup brined green olives, rinsed, pitted, and finely chopped

2 tablespoons red wine vinegar

$1/2$ teaspoon salt

$1/2$ teaspoon freshly ground black pepper

$1/2$ teaspoon dried oregano

1 Preheat an oven to 400°F. Coat the eggplant with about 1 teaspoon of the oil and put it in a baking dish. Bake it until it collapses a little and is completely tender and soft when pierced with a fork all the way to the middle, about 45 minutes.

2 Remove the eggplant from the oven and let it stand for about 5 minutes, then cut the eggplant in half. Scoop out and discard any large seed sacs, then scoop the flesh into a bowl. Using a fork, mash the flesh. Alternatively, remove it from the bowl, finely chop it, and then return it to the bowl. Add the tomatoes, onion, garlic, capers, olives, vinegar, salt, pepper, and oregano and mix well. Slowly dribble in the remaining olive oil to achieve a soft, spreadable texture. Serve at room temperature.

Cook this passel of oil-cured olives directly over the fire, and serve it in a rustic bowl along with a round of pastis, Provençal style, or with chilled retsina, Greek style.

GRILLED OLIVE APPETIZER makes about 2 cups

2 cups salt-cured black olives
2 teaspoons fresh rosemary or thyme leaves
$^1/_4$ cup extra-virgin olive oil

1 In a bowl, combine the olives, rosemary or thyme, and olive oil and turn to coat the olives. Let them stand for 30 minutes.

2 Prepare a medium-hot wood or charcoal fire in a grill, or preheat a gas grill.

3 Put the olives in a vegetable grilling basket and place it on the grill rack 6 to 8 inches above the fire. Grill the olives, stirring, just until they begin to darken and wrinkle a bit, 3 to 4 minutes.

4 Transfer to a bowl and let cool for a minute or two before serving.

A layered tricolor terrine—green, white, black—makes an attractive presentation for an aperitif buffet or for a first course. Serve it accompanied with crisp cracker bread or with slices cut from a baguette or other sturdy country loaf. A crisp Italian Prosecco makes a festive aperitif.

TERRINE of LAYERED GOAT CHEESE and OLIVES with FRESH THYME makes about 1 1/2 cups; serves 6

1/2 pound fresh goat cheese

1/2 cup milk or heavy cream, or as needed

2/3 cup brined green olives, rinsed, pitted, and chopped

2/3 cup salt-cured black olives, pitted and chopped

2 teaspoons fresh thyme leaves, minced

1 In a small bowl, combine the goat cheese and 1/2 cup milk or cream and mix to make a smooth, rather light spread. If it is too dense, add more milk or cream. Evenly spread about one-third of the cheese mixture in a glass terrine or bowl. It should be about 1 inch deep. Spread the green olives evenly over the surface in a layer about 1/2 inch deep. Top with half of the remaining cheese mixture and then the black olives. Finally, spread the remaining cheese mixture over the black olives, and sprinkle the surface with the thyme. Cover with plastic wrap and chill in the refrigerator for about 6 hours.

2 Bring to room temperature before serving.

appetizers and salads

Use the best-quality anchovies you can find and your finest extra-virgin olive oil for this classic Spanish tapa. Because the ingredients are so pure and so simple, the flavors of each are intensely apparent.

WHITE BEANS with ANCHOVIES serves 6

1 rounded cup (about $1/2$ pound) dried cannellini or other large
   white beans
5 cups water
$1/2$ teaspoon salt
1 dried bay leaf
3 tablespoons red wine vinegar
2 tablespoons extra-virgin olive oil
$1/2$ teaspoon freshly ground black pepper
15 or 16 olive oil–packed anchovy fillets, drained and each cut
   into 3 pieces
1 teaspoon minced fresh flat-leaf parsley

1 Rinse the beans. In a saucepan, combine them with 4 cups of the water, the salt, and the bay leaf. Bring to a boil, and then reduce the heat to low, cover, and cook for about 1 hour. Add the remaining 1 cup water and continue to cook until the beans are tender but still hold their shape, 1 to $1^1/_4$ hours longer. The time will vary depending upon the age of the beans.

2 Drain the beans and place in a shallow bowl. While they are still warm, add the vinegar, olive oil, pepper, and anchovies, turning gently to mix the ingredients and being careful not to break up or mash the tender beans.

3 At this point, the beans can be cooled to room temperature and then refrigerated for up to 3 or 4 days. Before serving, bring to room temperature and garnish with the parsley.

Romaine is a robustly flavored and sturdy lettuce that stands up to a thick dressing made with crushed anchovies. In Italy and southern France, you might find this salad served with a thick shaving of aged goat's or sheep's milk cheese, but I find the fresh cheese makes a lighter, yet equally tasty salad.

ANCHOVY, GOAT CHEESE, and ROMAINE SALAD   serves 4

2 large romaine hearts
1 or 2 cloves garlic
$1/4$ teaspoon coarse sea salt or kosher salt
8 to 10 anchovy fillets
$1/4$ cup extra-virgin olive oil
2 to 3 tablespoons red wine vinegar
$1/4$ teaspoon freshly ground black pepper
3 ounces fresh goat cheese
$1/4$ cup minced red onion

1 Cut the romaine hearts lengthwise into 1-inch-wide pieces and place in a bowl.

2 In a mortar, combine the garlic and salt and crush them together with a pestle to make a paste. (If you lack a mortar and pestle, use a bowl and a fork.) Add the anchovy fillets and crush them into the paste. Add the olive oil, vinegar, and pepper and mix together with a fork to make the dressing.

3 Drizzle the dressing over the romaine leaves and toss gently. Divide the lettuce equally among 4 salad plates. Dot each salad with bits of the goat cheese, then sprinkle each with a little red onion. Serve immediately.

In Collioure, the anchovy capital of southern France, anchovies are served as a first course Catalan style, liberally doused with a vinegar made from the region's famed sweet, slightly fortified wine, Banyuls.

CATALAN-STYLE ANCHOVIES   serves 4 to 6

2 red sweet peppers

12 anchovy fillets

6 hard-boiled eggs, peeled and halved lengthwise

2 cloves garlic, minced

$^1/_2$ cup minced fresh flat-leaf parsley

3 to 4 tablespoons extra-virgin olive oil

2 to 3 tablespoons *vinaigre de Banyuls* or other red wine vinegar

1 Preheat a broiler. Place the sweet peppers on a broiler tray and slide under the broiler. Broil, turning as necessary to color evenly, until blackened on all sides. Slip the peppers into a plastic bag and close the top. Let stand to allow the skin to steam and loosen, 4 to 5 minutes. Remove the peppers from the bag and peel off the blackened skin. Pull or cut away the stems, slit lengthwise, and remove the seeds and ribs. Cut into long strips $^1/_2$ inch wide.

2 Arrange the anchovy fillets, eggs, and pepper strips on a plate. Sprinkle the minced garlic and parsley over all. Drizzle all with the olive oil and the vinegar. Serve at once.

olives, anchovies, and capers

A potato salad prepared in the Mediterranean kitchen finds its character in the full-bodied flavors of anchovies and olives. Although capers are not included here, they would be good additions as well. Look for canned tuna packed in good-quality olive oil imported from Italy or elsewhere in the Mediterranean. It is generally moister and more flavorful (it is typically from the belly of the fish) than canned tuna from elsewhere (see Sources, page 126).

POTATO SALAD with TUNA, ANCHOVY, and OLIVES serves 6

8 waxy boiling potatoes such as Yukon Gold, White Rose, or Bintje,
 about 4 pounds total
2$^1/_2$ teaspoons salt
2 red sweet peppers
$^1/_4$ cup minced yellow onion
$^1/_3$ cup extra-virgin olive oil
$^1/_4$ cup red wine vinegar
1 teaspoon freshly ground black pepper
1 can (8 ounces) olive oil–packed tuna, drained and flaked
16 olive oil–packed anchovy fillets, drained and cut in half crosswise, plus 3 whole fillets for garnish
$^1/_2$ cup salt-cured black olives, pitted and chopped
4 hard-boiled eggs, peeled and sliced crosswise
1 tablespoon minced fresh flat-leaf parsley or basil

1 In a saucepan, combine the potatoes with water to cover by 2 inches. Bring to a boil over high heat and add 1 teaspoon of the salt. Reduce the heat to low and cook, uncovered, until the potatoes can be easily pierced with the tip of a sharp knife, about 20 minutes.

2 While the potatoes are cooking, preheat a broiler. Place the sweet peppers on a broiler tray and slide under the broiler. Broil, turning as necessary to color evenly, until blackened on all sides. Slip the peppers into a plastic bag and close the top. Let stand to allow the skin to steam and loosen, 4 to 5 minutes. Remove the peppers from the bag and peel off the blackened skin. Pull or cut away the stems, slit lengthwise, and remove the seeds and ribs. Cut into long, narrow strips.

3 When the potatoes are ready, drain them and, when cool enough to handle, peel them. Slice about $1/4$ inch thick and spread out on a platter.

4 In a small bowl, combine the onion, olive oil, vinegar, the remaining $1^1/2$ teaspoons salt, and the pepper and mix well. Pour the dressing over the potatoes, gently turning them to coat evenly. Add the strips of red pepper, the tuna, the halved anchovy fillets, and the olives and gently turn these with the potatoes and dressing, coating evenly. Add half of the egg slices and carefully turn them with the other ingredients. Arrange the remaining egg slices on the top of the salad, garnish with the whole anchovy fillets, and sprinkle with the parsley or basil. Serve warm or at room temperature.

The market in the Tunisian port city of Gabès is famous for its spices, but on a visit there late one afternoon I was also attracted to the huge burlap bags full of glistening sun-dried anchovies sold by weight. That evening I ate the pleasantly salty fish in a salad at a sophisticated, yet small and friendly restaurant. I have tried to re-create that dish here using salted anchovies.

ANCHOVY and GRILLED CHILE SALAD serves 4

2 fresh poblano chiles, or 1 green sweet pepper plus 2 serrano chiles

3 tablespoons extra-virgin olive oil

10 salted anchovies, rinsed, filleted, dried, and coarsely chopped

$1/4$ cup red wine vinegar

1 tablespoon minced fresh flat-leaf parsley

1 tablespoon minced fresh cilantro

1 teaspoon freshly ground black pepper

4 to 8 butterhead lettuce leaves

1 Seed the poblano chiles or the sweet pepper and serrano chiles and cut lengthwise into narrow strips. In a frying pan, heat the olive oil over medium heat. When it is hot, add the chiles or the sweet pepper and chiles and fry just until the edges begin to brown, 2 to 3 minutes. Using a slotted spoon, transfer them to a paper towel to drain for a minute or two, then place in a bowl.

2 Add the anchovies, vinegar, parsley, cilantro, and pepper to the bowl and mix well. Cover and refrigerate for at least 1 hour or up to overnight. Bring the salad to room temperature before serving.

3 Line 4 salad plates with the lettuce leaves, and spoon the salad evenly on top. Serve at once.

olives, anchovies, and capers

In the winter markets of Italy, Spain, and France, citrus fruits appear in profusion alongside the season's escarole and other chicories, a perfect pairing for salads. The capers and green olives deliver a pleasant bite to this combination of grapefruit, orange, and greens.

MIXED CITRUS SALAD with CAPERS and GREEN OLIVES serves 4

1 grapefruit

1 orange

2 cups escarole leaves, tender yellow inner leaves only, torn into bite-sized pieces

1 tablespoon capers, rinsed and drained

$1/3$ cup brined green olives, pitted and halved

3 tablespoons fresh lemon juice

$1/3$ cup extra-virgin olive oil

$1/4$ cup chopped fresh cilantro

1 On a cutting board, cut a thick slice off the top and bottom of the grapefruit to reveal the flesh. Stand the grapefruit upright and cut off the peel in wide strips, following the contour of the fruit and removing all the white membrane. Holding the grapefruit in one hand, cut along both sides of each segment to release it. Remove any seeds, then cut the segments into bite-sized pieces. Repeat with the orange.

2 In a bowl, combine the grapefruit and orange pieces and the escarole and turn to mix well. Add the capers and olives and turn again.

3 In a small bowl, whisk together the lemon juice, olive oil, and cilantro to make a dressing. Pour the dressing over the salad and turn again to mix well. Serve at once.

appetizers and salads

Oranges are used extensively in Mediterranean dishes, especially in the countries where they grow abundantly, such as Morocco, Tunisia, and Spain. They are frequently paired with contrasting savory flavors such as capers, anchovies, and olives. In this dish, 3 or 4 chopped anchovies or $1/3$ cup salt-cured black olives can be substituted for the capers.

FENNEL, ORANGE, and CAPER SALAD serves 4

3 oranges
1 large or 2 medium fennel bulbs
1 tablespoon minced fresh flat-leaf parsley
1 tablespoon capers, rinsed and drained
6 tablespoons extra-virgin olive oil
2 tablespoons sherry vinegar

1 Working with 1 orange at a time, on a cutting board, cut a thick slice off the top and bottom to reveal the flesh. Stand the orange upright and cut off the peel in wide strips, following the contour of the fruit and removing all the white membrane. Then cut the orange crosswise into generous $1/4$-inch-thick slices. Carefully remove any seeds. Arrange the slices on a platter.

2 Trim off the stems and any feathery leaves from the fennel bulbs. Using a mandoline if possible, cut the bulb lengthwise into paper-thin slices, then julienne the slices. Arrange the julienned fennel on top of the oranges, and sprinkle the parsley and capers over the top. Drizzle with the olive oil and vinegar. Cover and refrigerate for at least 1 hour or up to 6 hours, to allow the flavors to blend.

3 Serve slightly chilled or at room temperature.

Beans, although a New World food like tomatoes and squashes, have become firmly entrenched in Mediterranean cooking. This recipe is an adaptation of a dish I read about in a Spanish magazine.

GREEN BEAN and BLACK OLIVE SALAD

serves 4 to 6

1 pound young, tender green beans, trimmed

1 pound young, tender yellow wax beans, trimmed

2 teaspoons salt

4 or 5 fresh winter savory or thyme sprigs

1 teaspoon freshly ground black pepper

$1/2$ cup salt-cured black olives, pitted and coarsely chopped

2 tablespoons fresh lemon juice

$1/4$ cup extra-virgin olive oil

1 In a saucepan, combine the beans with water to cover by at least 2 inches. Add 1 teaspoon of the salt and 2 or 3 of the herb sprigs and bring to a boil over high heat. Reduce the heat to medium and cook the beans until they are tender to the bite, 3 to 5 minutes for young, tender beans, longer for more mature ones. Drain and immediately immerse in cold water to halt the cooking. Discard the herb sprigs. Drain the beans, pat dry, and place in a bowl.

2 Strip the leaves from the remaining herb sprigs and mince them. Add them to the beans along with the remaining 1 teaspoon salt, the pepper, and the olives. Turn to mix, then add the lemon juice and olive oil and mix again.

3 Serve the salad at room temperature.

olives, anchovies, and capers

This reminds me of a devilishly spicy potato salad I once ate in Sicily as part of an antipasto buffet. It was delicious with the grilled marinated sardines and sweet-and-sour eggplant I chose from the table as well, all of them accompanied with a big, white Sicilian wine.

NEW POTATO SALAD with CAPERS and RED PEPPER FLAKES serves 4

2 pounds new potatoes

2 teaspoons salt

1 teaspoon freshly ground black pepper

1 teaspoon red pepper flakes

3 tablespoons capers, rinsed and drained

1 tablespoon green peppercorns, rinsed and drained

2 tablespoons minced fresh basil

$1/4$ cup extra-virgin olive oil

1 to $1^1/2$ tablespoons red wine vinegar

1 In a saucepan, combine the potatoes with water to cover by 2 inches. Bring to a boil over high heat and add 1 teaspoon of the salt. Reduce the heat to low and cook, uncovered, until the potatoes are easily pierced with the tip of a sharp knife, about 20 minutes. Drain and, when just cool enough to handle, use a sharp knife to peel the potatoes. The skins, for the most part, will slip away easily.

2 Thinly slice the still-warm potatoes and put them in a large bowl, sprinkling the layers with the remaining 1 teaspoon salt, the black pepper, red pepper flakes, capers, peppercorns, basil, and some of the olive oil and vinegar. When all of the potatoes are in the bowl, add the remaining olive oil and vinegar and turn gently to coat the slices evenly.

3 Serve the salad at room temperature.

An abundance of fresh herbs and capers gives a slightly sharp flavor to this pasta salad, and the addition of tuna raises it to the status of a light main dish. To make a vegetarian version, substitute about $1/2$ cup chopped roasted red sweet peppers and $1/2$ cup salt-cured black olives, chopped, for the tuna.

PENNE SALAD with THREE HERBS, CAPERS, and TUNA serves 4

1 can (6 ounces) olive oil–packed tuna
$1^1/_2$ teaspoons salt
$1/_2$ pound penne
2 tablespoons fresh lemon juice
2 tablespoons extra-virgin olive oil
$1/_2$ teaspoon freshly ground black pepper
2 teaspoons capers, rinsed and drained
$1/_4$ cup chopped fresh flat-leaf parsley
$1/_4$ cup chopped fresh basil
$1/_4$ cup chopped fresh cilantro

1 Drain the tuna of as much of its oil as possible. Put it in a bowl and, using a fork, break it into flakes. Set aside.

2 Bring a large pot filled with water to a boil. Add 1 teaspoon of the salt and the penne, stir well, and cook until al dente, 10 to 12 minutes. The timing will depend upon the type of pasta. Drain well.

3 In a bowl, combine the still-hot penne, lemon juice, olive oil, the remaining $1/2$ teaspoon salt, and the pepper and mix well. Add the capers, parsley, basil, cilantro, and tuna and mix gently. Taste and adjust the seasoning. Cover and refrigerate for an hour or so before serving.

4 To serve, transfer the salad to a serving bowl or divide among individual plates. Serve at room temperature.

Rice dishes appear on tables throughout the Mediterranean basin, especially where rice has long been an important crop. This particular salad, however, is a recent invention of a Provençal friend. The rice absorbs the flavors of the local olives and capers, all richly seasoned with fresh herbs, olive oil, and vinegar. Use this recipe as a starting point from which to create your own Mediterranean-style rice salad.

RICE SALAD with OLIVES, CAPERS, and RED ONIONS serves 4 to 6

2 cups water

$1/2$ teaspoon salt

1 cup medium- or short-grain white rice

$1/4$ cup extra-virgin olive oil

$2 1/2$ tablespoons red wine vinegar

$1/2$ teaspoon ground cumin

3 tomatoes, peeled, seeded, and chopped

$1/2$ cup brined green olives, rinsed, pitted, and chopped or
    salt-cured black olives, pitted and chopped

$1/4$ cup capers, rinsed and drained

$1/4$ minced red onion

$1/4$ cup chopped fresh basil

1 teaspoon salt

1 teaspoon freshly ground black pepper

1 In a saucepan, combine the water and salt and bring to a boil over high heat. Add the rice and bring back to a boil. Reduce the heat to low, cover, and cook until the water has been absorbed and the rice is tender, about 20 minutes. Let the rice cool completely.

2 In a bowl, combine the rice, olive oil, vinegar, and cumin. Turn with a fork to season the rice and separate the grains. Add the tomatoes, olives, capers, onion, basil, salt, and pepper and gently turn to distribute the ingredients evenly.

3 Serve the salad at room temperature.

Although this salad originated in Nice, it is popular throughout France, and other Mediterranean countries have their own versions of fish and vegetable salads. The ingredient list is long, but the dish is simply an assembly of cooked and raw vegetables with tuna, egg, and anchovies dressed with a vinaigrette. Some purists hold that only uncooked vegetables and oil-packed canned tuna should be used, but I have become accustomed to this version prepared by Provençal friends, sometimes with grilled fresh tuna.

SALADE NIÇOISE   serves 6

1 pound boiling potatoes such as White Rose, Yukon Gold, or Bintje

1½ teaspoons salt

1 pound haricots verts or other thin green beans, trimmed

2 cups mixed young lettuce leaves

5 tomatoes, sliced ¼ inch thick

1 cucumber, peeled and sliced ¼ inch thick

4 hard-boiled eggs, peeled and sliced crosswise ¼ inch thick

16 anchovy fillets

1 can (8 ounces) olive oil–packed tuna

½ cup salt-cured black olives

¼ cup extra-virgin olive oil

2 tablespoons red wine vinegar

1 clove garlic, minced

½ teaspoon freshly ground black pepper

1 In a saucepan, combine the potatoes with water to cover by 2 inches. Add 1 teaspoon of the salt, bring to a boil, reduce the heat to medium, and cook, uncovered, until the potatoes can be easily pierced with the tip of a sharp knife, about 20 minutes. Drain and let cool, then peel and slice ¼ inch thick. Set aside.

2 Arrange the haricots verts or other beans on a steamer rack above boiling water, cover, and steam until barely tender, 2 to 3 minutes. Remove the beans from the steamer and immediately immerse in cold water to halt the cooking. Set aside.

continued

appetizers and salads

3 Line a serving platter with the lettuce leaves. Place the pota-toes, beans, tomatoes, cucumber, and eggs in attractive piles on top of the lettuce. Place the anchovy fillets atop the eggs and tomatoes. Drain the tuna and place it on the platter in a mound. Scatter the olives over all the elements.

4 In a bowl, whisk together the olive oil, vinegar, garlic, the remaining ¹/₂ teaspoon salt, and the pepper to make a vinaigrette. Pour the vinaigrette evenly over the salad and serve at once.

Smoky-tasting grilled fresh tuna and tangy capers and green peppercorns are mixed with classic tuna-salad ingredients to create a dish worthy of a special occasion. The tuna can be cooked a day ahead. I serve this as an appetizer on toasts.

SALAD OF GRILLED TUNA with CAPERS and GREEN PEPPERCORNS serves 4

1 tuna steak or fillet, about 10 ounces

2$^{1}/_{2}$ tablespoons capers, rinsed, drained, and chopped

1$^{1}/_{2}$ teaspoons pickled green peppercorns, drained and crushed

3 tablespoons grated yellow onion

$^{1}/_{2}$ teaspoon freshly ground black pepper

salt to taste

$^{1}/_{2}$ to $^{3}/_{4}$ cup mayonnaise, preferably homemade

4 large or 8 small red leaf or other attractive lettuce leaves

8 baguette slices, toasted

1 Prepare a medium-hot wood or charcoal fire in a grill, or preheat a gas grill.

2 When the fire is ready, place the tuna steak or fillet on the oiled grill rack and grill, turning once, until browned on the outside and rare at the center, about 3 minutes on each side. Remove from the grill and let cool slightly. Remove the skin, as well as the bone if using a tuna steak. Using a fork or your fingertips, flake the meat.

3 In a bowl, mix together the tuna, capers, peppercorns, onion, pepper, salt, and enough mayonnaise to bind the mixture. Line 4 salad plates with the lettuce leaves. Divide the salad among them, mounding it in the center.

4 Cover and chill, if desired, or serve at room temperature. Place 2 baguette slices on each plate just before serving.

This is not a typical dish of the Mediterranean, but the inclusion of the salt-cured olives is a perfect example of how the addition of a secret ingredient, along with some fresh herbs, can create a tantalizing dish.

HALIBUT SALAD with ORZO and BLACK OLIVES   serves 8

For the fish:

1½ pounds halibut fillet, cut into 1½-inch cubes (about 40 cubes)

1 tablespoon finely grated lemon zest

2 tablespoons fresh lemon juice

1 tablespoon extra-virgin olive oil

3 or 4 fresh mint sprigs

½ teaspoon salt

½ teaspoon freshly ground black pepper

For the orzo:

3 tablespoons fresh lemon juice

¼ cup extra-virgin olive oil

1 clove garlic, minced

1½ teaspoons salt

½ teaspoon freshly ground black pepper

2 quarts water

½ pound orzo

2 teaspoons finely grated lemon zest

½ cup salt-cured black olives, pitted and coarsely chopped

¼ cup chopped fresh mint

2 tablespoons minced fresh flat-leaf parsley

1 To prepare the fish, put the cubed halibut in a bowl and add the lemon zest, lemon juice, olive oil, mint sprigs, salt, and pepper. Turn the cubes to coat them. Cover and refrigerate for 20 to 30 minutes.

2 To prepare the orzo, in a bowl, combine the lemon juice, olive oil, garlic, ½ teaspoon of the salt, and the pepper and stir to mix.

continued

appetizers and salads

3 In a saucepan, bring the water to a boil over medium-high heat. Add the remaining 1 teaspoon salt and the orzo and cook until al dente, 4 to 5 minutes. Drain well and place in a bowl. Pour the lemon juice combination over the warm orzo and turn to coat. Gently turn in the lemon zest, olives, mint, and parsley. Cover to keep warm.

4 Prepare a medium-hot wood or charcoal fire in a grill, or preheat a gas grill or a broiler. Oil the grill rack, if grilling, or ready the broiler tray.

5 Thread the halibut cubes onto about 8 skewers. Do not pack them too tightly. Place the skewers on the grill rack 5 to 6 inches from the heat source, or in the broiler at about the same distance from the heat, and grill, turning once, for about 5 minutes on each side. The fish should be just opaque at the center. Do not overcook.

6 Remove the fish from the fire and let rest for about 10 minutes. Slide the fish from the skewers. Arrange the orzo on a platter, and top with the fish. Serve warm or at room temperature.

Lentils are an important ingredient in the Mediterranean pantry. Their nutty taste combines well with a number of foods, including olives and capers. Here, the lentils provide a flavorful backdrop for juicy duck breasts. To serve this salad as a main dish for brunch or lunch, accompany it with crispy fried polenta triangles or warm focaccia.

LENTIL and DUCK BREAST SALAD serves 5 or 6

3 teaspoons salt

$1/4$ teaspoon freshly ground black pepper

$1/2$ teaspoon dried oregano

$1/4$ teaspoon dried thyme

4 boneless duck breast halves

1 red sweet pepper

$1^{1}/2$ cups dried lentils, preferably small French green lentils, rinsed

5 cups water

2 fresh bay leaves, or 1 dried bay leaf

1 cup brined green olives, rinsed, pitted, and finely chopped

1 tablespoon capers, rinsed and drained

3 tablespoons extra-virgin olive oil

2 tablespoons balsamic vinegar

1 tablespoon chopped fresh flat-leaf parsley

1 In a bowl, combine 2 teaspoons of the salt with the pepper, oregano, and thyme. Rub the duck breasts all over with this mixture, then put them in a plastic bag and refrigerate overnight.

2 The next day, preheat a broiler. Place the pepper on a broiler tray and slide under the broiler. Broil, turning as necessary, until blackened on all sides. Slip the pepper into a plastic bag and close the top. Let stand to allow the skin to steam and loosen, 4 to 5 minutes. Remove the pepper from the bag and remove the blackened skin. Remove the stem, slit lengthwise, and remove the seeds and ribs. Cut 6 long, narrow strips from the pepper and set aside. Reserve the remaining pepper for another use.

3 In a saucepan, combine the lentils, water, the remaining

1 teaspoon salt, and the bay. Bring to a boil over medium-high heat, then reduce the heat to low and simmer, uncovered, until the lentils are tender to the bite, 20 to 25 minutes. Drain thoroughly, transfer to a bowl, and add the olives, capers, 2 tablespoons of the olive oil, and the vinegar. Mix well and set aside, covering to keep them warm.

4 In a skillet, heat the remaining 1 tablespoon olive oil over medium-high heat. Pat the duck breasts dry and place them, skin side down, in the hot oil. Reduce the heat to medium and cook, turning once, until browned on the outside but still rare in the center, 3 to 4 minutes on each side. Remove the duck breasts to a cutting board, cover loosely with aluminum foil, and let them rest for 5 minutes.

5 Thinly slice the duck breasts against the grain. Arrange the lentils on a serving platter. Lay the duck breast slices on top, fanning them slightly but maintaining the shape of each breast half. Top with the roasted pepper strips.

6 Sprinkle with the parsley and serve warm.

CHAPTER 2: | MAIN DISHES

In Mediterranean countries, omelets and other egg dishes are often served as a main course. This is an Italian example using Gorgonzola, but a Greek version might use feta and mint, and a North African one would likely combine sheep's milk cheese and a spicy red sauce.

OMELET OF TOMATOES and BLACK OLIVES with GORGONZOLA <small>serves 3 or 4</small>

$^1/_2$ pound tomatoes, peeled, seeded, and diced

$^1/_2$ teaspoon salt

1 teaspoon freshly ground black pepper

$^1/_4$ cup salt-cured black olives, pitted and coarsely chopped, plus several whole olives for garnish

6 eggs

2 tablespoons unsalted butter

1 ounce Gorgonzola cheese, cut into small pieces

1 In a bowl, combine the tomatoes, $^1/_4$ teaspoon of the salt, $^1/_2$ teaspoon of the pepper, and the chopped olives. Toss to mix. Set aside.

2 In another bowl, combine the eggs with the remaining $^1/_4$ teaspoon salt and $^1/_2$ teaspoon pepper. Beat lightly just until blended.

3 In a 12-inch skillet, melt the butter over medium heat. When it foams, add the eggs and stir until they begin to thicken, just a few seconds. Reduce the heat to low. As the eggs set along the edges, lift them with a spatula and tip the pan to let the uncooked egg run underneath. Continue to cook until the eggs are just set, 30 to 40 seconds. The timing will depend upon whether a slightly runny or a firm omelet is preferred. The bottom should be lightly golden.

4 Dot one-half of the omelet with the cheese, then add the tomato and olive mixture. Slip a spatula under the uncoated half and flip the uncovered half over the covered half. Cook until the cheese starts to melt, 30 to 40 seconds longer. Slide the omelet onto a warmed platter.

5 Cut into serving portions, garnish with whole olives, and serve immediately.

In this Italian favorite, the anchovies give the vegetables a hearty boost and a taste of the sea, making it a much more interesting and substantial dish than with the vegetables alone.

ANCHOVY, ROASTED RED PEPPER, and **BROCCOLI PASTA** serves 4

2 cups red sweet peppers
3 cups broccoli florets
1 teaspoon salt
$3/4$ pound dried hollow pasta such as penne or rotelli
4 tablespoons extra-virgin olive oil
2 cloves garlic, minced
12 anchovy fillets, coarsely chopped
1 teaspoon freshly ground black pepper

1 Preheat a broiler. Place the sweet peppers on a broiler tray and slide under the broiler. Broil, turning as necessary to color evenly, until blackened on all sides. Slip the peppers into a plastic bag and close the top. Let stand to allow the skin to steam and loosen, 4 to 5 minutes. Remove the peppers from the bag and peel off the blackened skin. Pull or cut away the stems, slit lengthwise, and remove the seeds and ribs. Cut into long, narrow strips and set aside.

2 Place the broccoli florets on a steamer rack over boiling water, cover, and steam until just tender to the bite and still bright green, 3 to 4 minutes. Transfer to a plate and cover to keep warm. Set aside.

3 Bring a large pot of water to a boil. Add the salt and the pasta, stir well, and cook until al dente, about 10 minutes. The timing will depend upon the type of pasta.

4 While the pasta is cooking, in a small skillet, heat 1 tablespoon of the olive oil over medium heat. Add the garlic and sauté just until it begins to color, about 2 minutes. Remove from the heat and add the remaining 3 tablespoons olive oil and the anchovies. Set aside. Meanwhile, slice the broccoli florets lengthwise into bite-size pieces.

5 When the pasta is ready, drain it and put it in a serving bowl. Add the anchovy mixture, turning to coat the pasta well. Add the broccoli, red peppers, and pepper. Serve immediately, turning the vegetables and pasta together at the table.

Beans and pasta belong to the Italian repertoire, but other ingredients can be added as well. I like not only the extra flavor the olives and spinach contribute, but also the brilliant colors they bring to the dish.

PASTA with CRANBERRY BEANS, SPINACH, and BLACK OLIVES   serves 4

1 1/2 to 2 pounds fresh cranberry beans or other shelling beans
1 3/4 teaspoons salt
1 dried bay leaf
2 or 3 fresh winter savory or thyme sprigs
3/4 pound dried fettuccine, spaghetti, or other long pasta
1/3 cup extra-virgin olive oil
2 cloves garlic, minced
4 cups stemmed spinach leaves, coarsely chopped
1/2 cup oil-cured black olives, pitted
1/2 teaspoon freshly ground black pepper

1 Shell the beans to yield about 1 cup. In a saucepan, combine the beans with water to cover by 2 inches. Add 3/4 teaspoon of the salt, the bay leaf, and the winter savory or thyme and bring to a boil over high heat. Reduce the heat to low and cook, uncovered, until tender, 15 to 20 minutes.

2 Bring a large pot filled with water to a boil. Add the remaining 1 teaspoon salt and the pasta, stir well, and cook until the pasta is al dente, 10 to 12 minutes. The timing will depend upon the type of pasta.

3 While the pasta is cooking, in a saucepan, heat the olive oil over medium heat. Add the garlic and sauté until lightly golden, about 1 minute. Add the spinach and the olives, stir well, and cook just until the spinach is wilted, 2 to 3 minutes. Add the pepper and the drained beans, turning all together to distribute the ingredients evenly.

4 Drain the pasta and put it in a warmed serving bowl or on a platter. Add the spinach mixture and turn to mix well. Serve immediately.

In early summer when fresh anchovies are plentiful, I like to buy a big batch and invite some friends over. I spread the table outside with white butcher paper and set out chilled bottles of white or rosé wine, lots of lemons, and loaves of crusty bread. The grill is nearby, and I pass the hot fish directly to the table. It's one of those hands-on meals that leads to lots of conviviality and conversation. Eating the small fish may seem a bit of a challenge at first, but the flavorful, firm flesh, full of the smoky taste of the grill, lifts cleanly away from the skeleton.

GRILLED FRESH ANCHOVIES with THYME
serves 4

vegetable oil
3 pounds fresh anchovies
1 teaspoon salt
2 teaspoons freshly ground black pepper
1 tablespoon fresh thyme leaves, minced
4 lemons, quartered

1 Prepare a medium-hot wood or charcoal fire in a grill, or preheat a gas grill.

2 Oil both the inside and outside of a long-handled grilling basket and lay as many anchovies in it as will fit in a single layer, spacing them at least $\frac{1}{2}$ inch apart. Sprinkle with some of the salt, pepper, and thyme. Close the top and fasten it securely.

3 Place the basket on the grill rack 6 to 8 inches from the fire and grill, turning once, until the meat flakes easily from the bone, 2 to 3 minutes on each side. Transfer the anchovies to a warmed platter and repeat until all the fish are cooked.

4 Serve immediately, accompanied with the lemons.

Olives are an excellent addition to Greek- and Turkish-style pilafs, bringing both flavor and color. This particular dish makes a nice vegetarian main course if vegetable broth is used, and could be accompanied with Caponata, Provençal Style (page 37) or perhaps a Greek salad of tomatoes, cucumbers, and onions.

ZUCCHINI and BLACK OLIVE PILAF   serves 4

1 zucchini

1 tablespoon unsalted butter

1 tablespoon extra-virgin olive oil

2 tablespoons minced yellow onion

$1/2$ teaspoon freshly ground black pepper

1 cup long-grain white rice

$1/4$ cup salt-cured black olives, pitted and chopped

1 tablespoon chopped fresh cilantro

2 cups vegetable or chicken broth

1 teaspoon salt

1 Grate the zucchini on the large holes of a handheld grater.

2 In a saucepan, melt the butter with the oil over medium-low heat. When the butter melts, add the onion and pepper and sauté until the onion is translucent, 2 to 3 minutes. Add the rice and cook, stirring occasionally, until opaque and coated with the butter and oil, 3 to 4 minutes longer. Add the olives, cilantro, and zucchini and cook, stirring, for about 30 seconds to blend the ingredients well.

3 Pour in the broth, add the salt, raise the heat to medium-high, and bring to a boil. Cover, reduce the heat to low, and cook until the rice is tender and has absorbed all of the broth, about 20 minutes. Remove from the heat and let rest, covered, for 5 minutes. Then fluff with a fork and serve.

Saffron, which is the dried stigma of a variety of crocus, is traditional in Mediterranean dishes such as paella and bouillabaisse, but it is also used in many other preparations both for its intense coloring and slightly bitter flavor. I've used it here in combination with anchovies to create a rich and colorful broth. Halibut or another firm-fleshed white fish can be used in place of the sea bass.

SAFFRON SEA BASS BOWL   serves 4

2 tablespoons extra-virgin olive oil
1 small yellow onion, minced
2 cloves garlic, minced
2 anchovy fillets
8 large, very ripe tomatoes, peeled, seeded, and coarsely chopped, or 1 can (16 ounces) plum (Roma) tomatoes and their juice, seeded and coarsely chopped
2 cups chicken broth
$1/3$ cup dry white wine
1 dried bay leaf
1 teaspoon fresh thyme leaves
$1/4$ cup chopped fresh flat-leaf parsley
$1/2$ teaspoon freshly ground black pepper
1 can (7 ounces) minced or chopped clams, drained with liquid reserved
pinch of saffron threads
1 pound sea bass fillet, cut into $1 1/2$- to 2-inch chunks
$1/2$ pound bay shrimp (optional)
$1/4$ cup chopped fresh cilantro

1 In a large saucepan, heat the olive oil over medium heat. Add the onion, garlic, and anchovies and sauté, stirring to dissolve the anchovies into the oil, for 3 to 4 minutes. Add the tomatoes and their juice, broth, wine, bay leaf, thyme, parsley, and pepper. Stir well, then add the clam liquid and the saffron. Bring to a boil, reduce the heat to low, cover, and simmer for 10 minutes to blend the flavors. Add the clams and sea bass and simmer just until the sea bass is opaque throughout, 2 to 3 minutes. Stir in the shrimp, if using.

2 Ladle into warmed bowls and garnish with the cilantro. Serve immediately.

This is a simple and intensely flavorful way to serve firm-fleshed fish steaks, and it readily demonstrates how capers and olives can create a simple, yet deeply satisfying, dish with little effort. If you like, add chopped salt-cured black or brined green olives with the capers, or use olives and tomatoes alone.

SWORDFISH with CAPERS and FRESH TOMATOES serves 4

1^1/$_2$ tablespoons extra-virgin olive oil

4 swordfish steaks, each about 6 ounces and ^{1}/$_2$ inch thick

1^1/$_2$ teaspoons salt

^{1}/$_2$ teaspoon freshly ground black pepper

^{1}/$_4$ cup dry white wine

3 tomatoes, peeled, seeded, and chopped

1 tablespoon capers, rinsed and drained

1 tablespoon minced fresh flat-leaf parsley

1 In a skillet, heat the olive oil over medium-high heat. Rub the fish steaks with 1 teaspoon of the salt and the pepper and place in the skillet. Cook, turning once, until golden brown, about 2 minutes on each side. Add the white wine and stir to scrape up any bits clinging to the bottom of the pan. Reduce the heat to low and top each steak with an equal amount of the tomatoes and capers. Sprinkle with the remaining ^{1}/$_2$ teaspoon salt. Cook until the fish is just opaque throughout, 2 to 3 minutes longer.

2 Transfer the fish to warmed plates or a platter and garnish with the parsley. Serve at once.

olives, anchovies, and capers

Fennel, which grows wild throughout the Mediterranean, is often paired with fish, as are capers. This stuffing holds its shape when cooked, and, if desired, can be removed intact from the cavity before serving, or the fish can be plated with the stuffing still in place.

BAKED ROCKFISH with CAPER and FENNEL STUFFING   serves 4

2 to 3 medium-sized fennel bulbs

$1/3$ cup freshly made fine dried bread crumbs

2 tablespoons finely chopped fresh flat-leaf parsley

1 teaspoon salt

1 teaspoon freshly ground black pepper

2 tablespoons fresh lime juice

1 tablespoon capers, rinsed, drained, and chopped

$1/4$ cup dry white wine

2 to 3 tablespoons extra-virgin olive oil

4 small rockfish or sea bass, each about $3/4$ pound, cleaned

1 Preheat an oven to 400°F.

2 Trim off the stems and any feathery leaves from the fennel bulbs, then remove any bruised areas. Mince the bulbs and place in a mixing bowl. Add the bread crumbs, parsley, $1/2$ teaspoon each of the salt and pepper, the lime juice, and the capers. Mix well. Add the white wine and about 2 tablespoons of the olive oil. If the stuffing seems too crumbly, add a little more olive oil, just enough to hold the stuffing together.

3 Rub the fish inside and out with the remaining olive oil, salt, and pepper. Fill the fish cavities brimful with the stuffing and sew them shut with kitchen string. Place the fish on a baking sheet. Roast until the flesh bounces back when pressed, 10 to 12 minutes. Remove from the oven and clip and remove the strings, then serve.

Salt cod is such a common ingredient in the Mediterranean diet that many versions of deep-fried salt cod cakes exist. Here, a scattering of capers could be substituted for the olives, and the addition of a dash of red pepper flakes will deliver a spicy version. Salt cod needs to be desalted and refreshed before using, so begin making these cakes a day before serving.

SALT COD and OLIVE CAKES makes about 24 cakes; serves 4

$^1/_2$ pound salt cod

1 dried bay leaf

1 clove garlic, minced

1 teaspoon extra-virgin olive oil, if using a food processor, plus 1 tablespoon

1 cup all-purpose flour

1 teaspoon baking powder

$^3/_4$ cup water

1 yellow onion, minced

$^1/_4$ cup pitted and chopped brined green olives

1 tablespoon minced fresh flat-leaf parsley

1 teaspoon freshly ground black pepper

pure olive oil for deep-frying

2 lemons, cut into wedges

1 To refresh the salt cod, rinse it under running cold water for 10 minutes, then place in a bowl with water to cover. Cover and refrigerate for 24 hours, changing the water 2 or 3 times. Cut off a small piece, put it in a saucepan or small skillet with water to cover, and simmer for 3 to 4 minutes. Drain and taste for saltiness. It should not be bland, but instead pleasantly salty. If it is still too salty, continue to soak and sample the salt cod until the saltiness is pleasing to your taste.

2 Drain the soaked cod and place in a shallow pan. Add water to cover and the bay leaf. Bring to a gentle simmer and poach just until the fish flakes when pierced with a fork, 3 to 4 minutes. Remove the cod from the water and let cool.

3 Remove and discard any bones or skin from the fish, then squeeze dry. Put the fish and the garlic in a mortar and crush it to a purée with a pestle, or purée them in a food processor along with the 1 teaspoon olive oil. Set aside.

4 In a bowl, stir together the flour, baking powder, water, and the 1 tablespoon olive oil. The mixture should have the consistency of a thick cream. Add the cod mixture, onion, olives, parsley, and pepper to the flour mixture and mix well, adding more water if necessary to create a thick, pasty consistency.

5 In a deep fryer or deep, heavy-bottomed pot, pour in the pure olive oil to a depth of 4 inches and heat to 375°F. When the oil is ready, drop the cod mixture by the heaping tablespoon into the hot oil, adding only a few at a time so as not to crowd the pan. Cook until puffed and golden, 3 to 4 minutes. Using a slotted spoon, transfer the cakes to paper towels to drain. Keep warm. Repeat until all the cod mixture is used.

6 Arrange the cakes on a warmed platter and serve immediately with the lemon wedges.

This is one of my favorite quick meals to prepare year-round. A supply of capers and peppercorns are always in my refrigerator, and good-quality fresh salmon can now be counted on most of the year. I usually serve the fish with steamed spinach, a green salad, and a crisp white wine.

PAN-SEARED SALMON with CAPERS and GREEN PEPPERCORNS serves 4

1 teaspoon salt

4 salmon fillets, each about 6 ounces and $1/2$ inch thick

$1/2$ teaspoon freshly ground black pepper

$1/2$ cup dry white wine

$1/2$ cup fresh lemon juice

3 tablespoons water

2 tablespoons capers, rinsed and drained

1 tablespoon brine-packed green peppercorns

1 Sprinkle the salt in a heavy skillet and heat over medium-high heat until nearly smoking. Add the salmon and sear for about 2 minutes, then turn and sear on the other side for about 2 minutes. Reduce the heat to low, sprinkle with the pepper, and then pour in the wine and 2 tablespoons of the lemon juice. Cover and cook until the liquid is nearly absorbed, another 3 to 4 minutes.

2 Uncover and pour in 2 more tablespoons of the lemon juice and 2 tablespoons of the water. Re-cover and cook just until the fish is opaque throughout, 3 to 4 minutes. Transfer the salmon to warmed individual plates or a platter.

3 Add the remaining 4 tablespoons lemon juice and 1 tablespoon water and stir to scrape up any bits clinging to the bottom of the pan. Add the capers and peppercorns and cook, stirring, for about 30 seconds. Pour the pan juices evenly over the salmon and serve at once.

This recipe comes from chef Seen Lippert, formerly of the celebrated Chez Panisse, in Berkeley, California. We met on a trip to Spain and while we were talking about interesting low-fat ways to prepare fish, she shared this recipe with me. During the cooking, the anchovies dissolve slightly, lending subtle flavor to the cod and making beautiful dark bands against the pure white meat.

ROAST COD LARDED with ANCHOVIES   serves 4

1 teaspoon plus 2 tablespoons olive oil
1 teaspoon minced fresh rosemary
1 teaspoon freshly ground black pepper
1 large cod fillet, about $1^1/_2$ pounds and 1 to $1^1/_2$ inches
    thick, with skin intact
8 anchovy fillets

1 Preheat an oven to 500°F. Oil the bottom of a baking dish just large enough to hold the cod with the 1 teaspoon olive oil.

2 In a small bowl, combine the 2 tablespoons olive oil, the rosemary, and the pepper and mix well. Rub the cod all over with the oil mixture. Make 8 evenly spaced slits, each one a generous $^1/_4$ inch deep and about 3 inches long, in the surface of the fillet. Push an anchovy fillet into each slit. Place the fillet in the prepared baking dish.

3 Bake the fish until it is just opaque throughout and springs back when gently pushed, 15 to 20 minutes.

4 Remove from the oven and cut into 4 equal pieces, each with 2 of the anchovy-stuffed slits.

Rather than contributing their own flavor, the anchovies here intensify the flavor of the mustard and at the same time mellow its pungency. When the chicken is done, the mustard-anchovy spread will have baked to form a soft, golden brown crust, but there will be no hint of the otherwise distinctive taste of anchovy.

ROAST CHICKEN with MUSTARD-ANCHOVY CRUST serves 4

$^1/_4$ cup Dijon mustard
1 tablespoon extra-virgin olive oil
2 cloves garlic, minced
6 to 8 olive oil–packed anchovy fillets, minced
$^1/_2$ teaspoon freshly ground black pepper
1 chicken, $3^1/_2$ to 4 pounds

1 Preheat an oven to 350°F.

2 In a small bowl, combine the mustard, olive oil, garlic, anchovies, and pepper. Using a fork, mix into a paste. Rinse the chicken, pat dry, and place on a rack in a roasting pan. Using a spoon or a pastry brush, spread the paste in a thick coat over the chicken.

3 Roast the chicken until the juices run clear when the inner thigh is pierced with the tip of a sharp knife, or an instant-read thermometer inserted into the thigh away from the bone registers 180°F, about $1^1/_4$ hours. Remove from the oven, cover loosely with aluminum foil, and let rest for 5 to 10 minutes.

4 Carve the chicken into serving pieces and arrange in a warmed platter. Serve immediately.

My first couscous was eaten in Paris on the rue du Roi-de-Sicile, in a small hole-in-the-wall restaurant with no name on it. I had chicken and vegetables, mostly carrots and zucchini. It was a memorable occasion, not only for the food, but also the company. I was taken there by a friend's father and one of his friends, cronies from their army intelligence days together during World War II. This is my updated version of that long-ago chicken couscous.

GREEN OLIVE and ALMOND COUSCOUS with CARROT and CUMIN CHICKEN serves 4 or 5

For the chicken:

$1/2$ cup slivered blanched almonds

2 tablespoons extra-virgin olive oil

$1/2$ yellow onion, minced

2 cloves garlic, minced

2 pounds skinless chicken thighs

4 carrots, peeled and very thinly sliced

1 teaspoon ground cumin

$1/2$ teaspoon cayenne pepper

$1/2$ teaspoon salt

1 tablespoon all-purpose flour

$1/2$ teaspoon freshly ground black pepper

1 teaspoon fresh thyme leaves, minced

2 cups chicken broth

2 tablespoons tomato paste

For the couscous:

2 scant cups water

1 tablespoon unsalted butter

$1/2$ teaspoon salt

2 cups instant couscous

1 cup brined green olives, rinsed, pitted, and coarsely chopped

1 Preheat an oven to 450°F. Spread the almonds on a baking sheet and put them in the oven to toast, stirring often, until golden and fragrant, 7 to 8 minutes. Remove from the oven and set aside.

2 In a large, deep, heavy-bottomed skillet, heat the olive oil over medium heat. Add the onion and sauté until translucent, 2 to 3 minutes. Add the garlic and the chicken and sauté until the chicken is lightly browned on the first side, about 5 minutes. Turn and sauté on the other side until lightly browned, then add the carrots and sauté for another 2 to 3 minutes, turning the carrots and the chicken. Sprinkle the cumin, cayenne, salt, flour, and pepper evenly over the contents of the skillet. Add the minced thyme and stir to brown the flour. Slowly add the broth, stirring and scraping up any bits clinging to the bottom of the pan. Stir in the tomato paste, and when fully incorporated, cover and reduce the heat to low. Simmer for 5 minutes, then uncover and continue to cook until the chicken is tender and the sauce has thickened, about 10 minutes longer.

3 Just before the chicken is ready, prepare the couscous: In a saucepan, combine the water, butter, and salt and bring to a boil over medium heat. Pour in the couscous and return to a boil, then remove immediately from the heat. Cover and let stand for 5 minutes. Uncover and fluff with a fork, adding the olives as you fluff.

4 Transfer the chicken and sauce and the couscous to warmed separate bowls or platters and serve immediately.

Capers and Parmesan are an enviable combination. Here that pairing is folded into light, fluffy dumplings that cook in an earthy, homemade chicken soup.

HOMEMADE CHICKEN SOUP with CAPER and PARMESAN DUMPLINGS serves 5 or 6

For the soup:

1 chicken, about 4 pounds

2 carrots, halved

6 celery stalks, halved

6 black peppercorns

6 fresh flat-leaf parsley sprigs

1 dried bay leaf

3 or 4 fresh thyme sprigs

8 quarts water

1 teaspoon salt

$1/2$ teaspoon freshly ground black pepper

For the dumplings:

$1 1/2$ cups all-purpose flour

$2 1/4$ teaspoons baking powder

$1/2$ teaspoon salt

$1/2$ cup grated Parmesan cheese

$3/4$ cup milk

2 tablespoons capers, rinsed and drained

2 tablespoons chopped fresh flat-leaf parsley for garnish

1 Rinse the chicken and pat dry. In a soup pot, combine the chicken, carrots, celery, peppercorns, parsley, bay, thyme, and water. Bring to a boil over medium-high heat, then cover and reduce the heat to low. Simmer until the chicken meat moves easily from the bones, about 1 hour.

2 Transfer the chicken to a colander or large sieve set over a bowl. Remove the skin and meat from the bones. Cover and refrigerate the

continued

meat until needed and return the skin and bones to the soup pot. Continue to cook, uncovered, for another 2 hours to create a well-flavored broth. Remove from the heat and, using a spoon, skim off the fat from the surface.

3 Strain the broth, discarding the vegetables. You should have about 8 cups. Put the broth in a clean saucepan and bring to a simmer over medium-high heat. Add the salt and pepper.

4 Meanwhile, make the dumplings: Sift together the flour, baking powder, and salt into a bowl. Stir in the Parmesan. Add the milk and the capers all at once, stirring vigorously just long enough to mix the ingredients.

5 Tear or chop the chicken into bite-sized pieces.

6 When the broth is at a simmer, add the chicken pieces to the pan. Dip a tablespoon into the simmering broth, then scoop up a table-spoon of the dumpling batter. Using your finger, push it off the spoon into the broth. Repeat until all the batter is in the pan. Cover the pan, bring to a medium boil, and boil until the dumplings are cooked through, about 12 minutes.

7 Ladle the soup and dumplings into bowls and garnish with the parsley. Serve immediately.

Here, a few capers added at the end deliver a sharp burst of flavor that contrasts with the mellowness of a slow-cooked stew.

LAMB STEW with TOMATOES, SWEET PEPPERS, and CAPERS   serves 4 to 6

$^{1}/_{2}$ cup all-purpose flour

$1^{1}/_{2}$ pounds boneless lamb shoulder, cut into 1-inch cubes

2 tablespoons extra-virgin olive oil

1 tablespoon unsalted butter

3 cloves garlic, minced

$^{2}/_{3}$ cup dry red wine

$1^{1}/_{2}$ cups canned plum (Roma) tomatoes and their juice,
coarsely chopped

$^{1}/_{2}$ teaspoon salt

$^{1}/_{2}$ teaspoon freshly ground black pepper

20 fresh sage leaves

1 large or 2 medium-sized red sweet peppers, seeded and
cut lengthwise into strips about $^{1}/_{2}$ inch wide

2 tablespoons capers, rinsed and drained

1 Spread the flour on a plate and roll the lamb cubes in it, coating evenly. In a heavy-bottomed pan, heat the olive oil and butter over medium heat. Add the garlic and sauté briefly, about 1 minute. Remove with a slotted spoon. Raise the heat to medium-high, add the lamb pieces, and brown them lightly, a few at a time. Work in batches to avoid crowding the pan. As the pieces are ready, transfer them to a plate. When all of the meat has been browned, add the wine to the pan a little at a time, stirring to scrape up the bits clinging to the bottom. Add the tomatoes and return the meat and any collected juices to the pan along with the sautéed garlic, salt, pepper, and sage. Bring to a simmer, then reduce the heat to low, cover, and cook, stirring often, for about 45 minutes. Add the red peppers and continue to cook, stirring often, until the meat is tender, about 35 minutes. Add the capers and cook for another 10 minutes.

2 Transfer the stew to a serving dish and serve immediately.

main dishes

93

When cooked slowly, veal shanks are exceedingly tender and flavorful, and the sweet, rich marrow of the shank bone is the first thing I eat, being a lover of this delicacy. The parsnips cook to a luscious golden brown, and they, too, are surprisingly sweet. Capers, added at the end of the cooking, help to balance the overall taste of the dish by adding some acidity, a good example of using a secret ingredient.

VEAL SHANKS BRAISED with PARSNIPS serves 4

2 tablespoons unsalted butter
2 large leeks, including one-third of the greens, sliced $1/2$ inch thick
2 cloves garlic, minced
3 tablespoons extra-virgin olive oil
$1/2$ cup all-purpose flour
4 pieces veal shank, each about $1^1/2$ inches thick
    (about 2 pounds total)
1 teaspoon salt
1 teaspoon freshly ground black pepper
$1/2$ cup dry sherry or dry white wine
1 cup beef broth, or as needed
$1/2$ teaspoon fresh thyme or winter savory leaves, minced
1 dried bay leaf
3 or 4 parsnips, peeled and cut into 2-inch pieces
1 tablespoon capers, rinsed and drained

1 Preheat an oven to 350°F.

2 In a heavy-bottomed, ovenproof Dutch oven or other pot just large enough to hold the shanks in a single layer, melt the butter over medium heat. Add the leeks and garlic and sauté just until soft and translucent, 3 to 4 minutes. Remove the pot from the heat and set aside.

3 In a large skillet, heat the olive oil over medium-high heat. At the same time, spread the flour on a sheet of waxed paper and roll the veal shanks in it, coating evenly. Sprinkle the shanks with half of the salt and pepper. When the oil is hot, add the shanks, in batches if necessary, and cook until browned and crisp on all sides, about 10 minutes. Return the pot holding the leeks to medium heat and, using a slotted spoon, transfer the shanks to it, arranging them on top in a single layer.

4 Pour off all but about 1 tablespoon of the fat in the skillet, then return it to medium-high heat. Add the sherry and stir to scrape up any bits clinging to the bottom of the pan. Add the 1 cup broth, the thyme or savory, the bay leaf, and the remaining salt and pepper. Bring to a boil, then pour the mixture over the leeks and shanks.

5 Cover with a tight-fitting lid and place the pot in the oven. Cook, basting the meat every 20 minutes or so with the pot juices, for about $1^{1}/_{4}$ hours. If the liquid evaporates to within an inch or so, add a little more beef broth. Add the parsnips, turning them in the liquid, and continue to cook and baste for about 30 minutes longer. The dish is ready when the veal pulls easily from the bone and the tines of a fork meet little resistance when thrust into a piece of parsnip.

6 Remove from the oven and stir in the capers. Transfer to a warmed platter and serve hot.

In this Italian-inspired recipe, a golden crust of Parmesan seals in the meat juices, and lemon and capers offset the richness of the meat and cheese. This is one of my favorite preparations for veal chops, one I use frequently whenever I can find the thick, juicy chops like those that seem so readily available in France and Italy. For this dish, the tiny, nonpareil capers make the nicest presentation, but the big juicy capers like the ones sold in the markets in Sicily taste even better than the little ones. For a complete meal, serve the chops with steamed chard and garlicky mashed potatoes. The veal-lemon-caper trio is used in German schnitzel as well.

PARMESAN-CRUSTED VEAL CHOPS
FINISHED with LEMON and CAPERS   serves 4

$^1/_3$ cup grated Parmesan cheese

$^1/_2$ cup freshly made fine dried bread crumbs

1 teaspoon salt

$^1/_2$ teaspoon freshly ground black pepper

1 egg

1 teaspoon water

$^1/_4$ cup all-purpose flour

4 veal chops, each about 6 ounces and $^1/_2$ inch thick

$^1/_4$ cup all-purpose flour

5 tablespoons extra-virgin olive oil

juice of 2 lemons (about $^1/_3$ cup)

3 tablespoons capers, rinsed and drained

1 In a shallow bowl, combine the cheese, bread crumbs, salt, and pepper and mix well. In another shallow bowl, whisk together the egg and water just until blended. Spread the flour on a plate. Coat a veal chop on both sides with the flour, tapping off the excess. Dip the chop into the egg mixture, then dip it into the cheese mixture, coating it on both sides. Set the chop aside on waxed paper and quickly repeat with the remaining 3 chops.

2 In a heavy-bottomed skillet, heat the olive oil over medium heat. When it is hot, add the chops and fry, turning once, until a golden

continued

main dishes

crust has formed on the exterior, 2 to 3 minutes on each side. If the chops are browning too quickly, reduce the heat to low. Cover and cook until cooked through but still faintly pink at the center, 3 to 4 minutes. Transfer to a warmed platter or individual plates and keep warm.

3 Pour off all but 1 teaspoon of the oil from the skillet. Return the pan to medium-high heat, add the lemon juice, and stir to scrape up any bits clinging to the bottom of the pan. Reduce the heat to low, add the capers, and cook, stirring, for about 30 seconds.

4 Pour the lemon juice and capers evenly over the chops and serve immediately.

In Sicily, anchovy butter is used with baked sardines, and in Greece it flavors fish cooked in grape leaves. Despite the fact that one doesn't typically think of a fish garnish or fish butter on meat, anchovy butter is delicious with beef. The briny flavor and creamy texture of the cured fish blend well with butter, and a heaping tablespoon of the mixture melts atop a just-off-the-grill steak, flavoring it provocatively.

GRILLED HERBED STEAKS with ANCHOVY BUTTER   serves 4

1 tablespoon extra-virgin olive oil
4 salt-packed anchovies, filleted, rinsed, and minced
$^1/_4$ cup unsalted butter, at room temperature
1 teaspoon dry sherry
4 rib steaks, each about $^1/_2$ inch thick
1 tablespoon minced fresh thyme
1 tablespoon freshly ground black pepper

1 In a small skillet, combine the olive oil and the anchovy fillets and place over medium heat. Using a fork, mash the anchovies into the oil until they break apart and "melt." Remove from the heat.

2 In a blender or small food processor, combine the butter, anchovy mixture, and sherry and blend until smooth. Remove the anchovy butter to a piece of aluminum foil or waxed paper, shape it into a log, wrap, and refrigerate.

3 Prepare a medium-hot wood or charcoal fire in a grill, or preheat a gas grill.

4 Sprinkle the steaks on both sides with the thyme and pepper. When the fire is ready, place the steaks on the grill rack and grill, turning once, for 4 to 5 minutes on each side for medium-rare.

5 Transfer the steaks to individual plates, top each one with a generous 1-tablespoon slice of the butter, and serve immediately.

main dishes

Toward the end of the slow cooking of this ragout typical of the Avignon region in southern France, black olives are added to the pan, where they contribute a richness to the sauce as well as bring their own character and texture to the dish.

BEEF RAGOUT with BLACK OLIVES serves 6

$2^{1}/_{2}$ pounds boneless beef chuck

2 tablespoons extra-virgin olive oil

$^{1}/_{4}$ cup minced yellow onion

2 cloves garlic, minced

8 large, ripe tomatoes, peeled and coarsely chopped, or 1 can (16 ounces) plum (Roma) tomatoes and their juice, coarsely chopped

2 teaspoons fresh thyme leaves, minced

2 fresh bay leaves, or 1 dried bay leaf

1 teaspoon freshly ground black pepper

2 green sweet peppers, seeded and cut into 1-inch squares

$^{1}/_{3}$ cup salt-cured black olives, pitted or unpitted

1 Cut the meat into generous 2-inch pieces, as they will shrink during cooking. In a heavy-bottomed pan, heat the olive oil over medium-high heat. When it is hot, add the meat, in batches, and brown well on all sides, about 10 minutes. Using a slotted spoon, transfer the meat to a plate and set it aside.

2 Add the onion and garlic to the oil remaining in the pan, reducing the heat to medium, and sauté just until barely translucent, about 1 minute. Add the tomatoes and stir to scrape up any bits clinging to the bottom of the pan. Return the meat and any collected juices to the pan and add the thyme, bay, and pepper. Bring to a boil over medium-high heat, then reduce the heat to low, cover, and cook until the meat is tender enough to be cut with a fork, $1^{1}/_{2}$ to 2 hours.

3 Add the green peppers and continue to cook for 10 minutes. Then add the olives and cook until the peppers are tender and the olives have released their flavor, about 5 minutes longer.

4 Spoon onto plates and serve at once.

olives, anchovies, and capers

As is the case with so many classic dishes, *tapenade*, a specialty of southern France, comes in dozens of versions, and any kind of olive can be used. Sometimes bread crumbs or ground almonds are added for thickening, mustard is mixed in for a sharp flavor, or various herbs, such as thyme or rosemary, are used to deliver a hint of the woods. In its simplest application, *tapenade* is spread on toasts and served as an appetizer with aperitifs, from Champagne to sweet vermouth. It is also used as a sauce for vegetables and grilled meats and to flavor other foods such as pastas, stuffings, and flans.

TAPENADE makes about 1 cup

$1^1/_2$ cups (about $^1/_2$ pound) salt-cured black olives, pitted
16 anchovy fillets
3 tablespoons capers, rinsed and drained
$^1/_2$ teaspoon minced fresh thyme
1 to 2 tablespoons extra-virgin olive oil

1 Traditionally, this spread is made with a mortar and pestle, pounding the ingredients until they form a smooth paste. The process can also be accomplished in a blender, however. Put the olives, anchovies, capers, and thyme in a blender along with the olive oil and purée until smooth.

2 If you are not using it immediately, put the purée in a jar, cover tightly, and store in the refrigerator, where it will keep for up to 3 months.

Anchoïade, a thick to middling-thick Provençal pomade of pure anchovy flavor heightened by garlic, is not for the timid. It is spread onto toasts at aperitif time, or offered as a dipping sauce for raw vegetables such as fennel, carrots, celery, black radishes, and celery root. To serve it as a sauce, simply put it in a bowl surrounded by the vegetables, or pour it into individual bowls for each person.

ANCHOÏADE   makes about ³/₄ cup

6 cloves garlic, coarsely chopped
16 anchovy fillets
4 or 5 flat-leaf parsley sprigs
1 tablespoon red wine vinegar
$^1/_3$ to $^1/_2$ cup extra-virgin olive oil

Coarsely chop the garlic and the anchovies. Using a mortar and pestle, small food processor, or blender, mash or process the garlic, anchovies, and parsley, with the vinegar until blended together, then slowly add the olive oil, continuing until a thick paste forms. It will keep, covered, in the refrigerator for up to 1 week.

Caper butter is wonderful to have on hand for quick seasoning, and it is easy to make. Cut off slices of this flavored butter to top poached or grilled fish, boiled potatoes, grilled
asparagus, baked tomatoes, or eggplant. You can also stir a
slice or two into scrambled eggs or spread on toast.

CAPER BUTTER makes about ½ cup

½ cup unsalted butter, at room temperature
2 tablespoons capers, rinsed and drained

1 Using a wooden spoon or an electric mixer, soften the butter
in a bowl. Add the capers and mix until well blended. Shape the butter
into a log and wrap it in plastic wrap or aluminum foil. Store in the refrigerator for up to 1 week.

2 To use, cut off slices of the butter as needed.

spreads, sauces, and breads

Ravigote, a caper-and-green-herb-flavored sauce, can be made with a *velouté* (white sauce) base and served hot, or it can be made as it is here, with a vinaigrette base and served cold. Use this piquant sauce dished up on the side to accompany fish, potatoes, or boiled meats such as *bollito misto*, tongue, or cheeks.

RAVIGOTE SAUCE makes about 1 cup

$^{1}/_{4}$ cup Champagne vinegar or white wine vinegar

1 shallot, minced

1 heaping tablespoon capers, rinsed, drained, and chopped

2 cornichons, finely chopped

$^{1}/_{2}$ cup chopped fresh flat-leaf parsley

1 tablespoon chopped fresh chervil

1 tablespoon chopped fresh chives

$^{1}/_{4}$ teaspoon salt

$^{1}/_{4}$ teaspoon freshly ground black pepper

$^{1}/_{2}$ cup extra-virgin olive oil

Put the vinegar in a bowl and add the shallot. Let stand for 5 minutes or so. Add the capers, cornichons, parsley, chervil, chives, salt, and pepper and stir together with a fork. Stir in the olive oil, then taste and adjust with salt and pepper. It will keep, covered, in the refrigerator for up to 1 week.

In this recipe, parsley offers a clean, fresh flavor quite different from the more perfumed basil typically used in pesto. If desired, add additional anchovies for a stronger presence. Use the sauce on pasta, spooned into soups or stews, or lightly spread over vegetables such as green beans, beets, or potatoes. To make a thicker spread, to use on sandwiches for example, reduce the olive oil by 1 to 2 tablespoons.

PARSLEY and ANCHOVY PESTO makes about 1 cup

1 cup fresh flat-leaf parsley leaves
6 olive oil–packed anchovy fillets, coarsely chopped
1 clove garlic, chopped
$1/_4$ cup extra-virgin olive oil, or as needed
$1/_4$ cup grated Parmesan cheese
1 tablespoon fresh lemon juice
2 tablespoons pine nuts
salt to taste

Combine the parsley leaves, anchovies, garlic, and olive oil in a blender or food processor. Purée until smooth. Add the cheese, lemon juice, nuts, and salt and process until all the ingredients are well blended into a sauce. If the sauce seems too thick, add a little more olive oil.

Capers added to the classic French *velouté* sauce just before serving turns it into a traditional caper sauce. I've changed it a little, adding onion and tarragon to give it more of a tang. The sauce complements chicken, potatoes, carrots, or poached fish.

CAPER-ONION SAUCE   makes about 1¹/₂ cups

3 tablespoons unsalted butter

2 tablespoons all-purpose flour

¹/₂ teaspoon salt

¹/₂ teaspoon freshly ground black pepper

1³/₄ cups chicken broth, homemade or purchased

2 tablespoons minced yellow or white onion

1 cup dry white wine

2 tablespoons capers, rinsed and drained

1 tablespoon chopped fresh tarragon

1 In a heavy-bottomed saucepan, melt 2 tablespoons of the butter over medium-high heat. When it foams, remove from the heat and whisk in the flour, salt, and pepper to make a paste. Return to medium-high heat and gradually pour in the chicken broth, continuing to whisk all the while. When the broth is blended in, reduce the heat to low and simmer, stirring occasionally, until the sauce has thickened and there is no taste of flour, 15 to 20 minutes.

2 In a saucepan, melt the remaining 1 tablespoon butter over medium-high heat. When it foams, add the onion and sauté until translucent, 2 to 3 minutes. Add the wine and cook until it is reduced to about ¹/₂ cup, about 5 minutes. Stir in the capers and cook for another 1 to 2 minutes.

3 Stir the caper mixture and the tarragon into the thickened sauce and cook gently for a minute or two. Serve hot.

Nowhere is the marriage of anchovies, capers, olives, and tomatoes more felicitous than in the *puttanesca*, or street walker's sauce, of Naples. It is traditionally tossed with spaghetti, but it is also wonderful served with grilled fish such as tuna or swordfish.

PUTTANESCA SAUCE   makes about 3 cups

3 tablespoons extra-virgin olive oil

2 cloves garlic, minced

1 teaspoon red pepper flakes

1 cup salt-cured black olives, pitted and coarsely chopped

8 anchovy fillets, coarsely chopped

1 teaspoon fresh oregano or thyme leaves, minced

$1^{1}/_{2}$ pounds very ripe, juicy tomatoes, peeled and coarsely chopped, or 1 (28-ounce) can plum (Roma) tomatoes and their juice, coarsely chopped

2 tablespoons minced fresh flat-leaf parsley

3 tablespoons capers, rinsed and drained

$^{1}/_{4}$ teaspoon freshly ground black pepper

salt if needed

1 In a large skillet, heat the olive oil over medium heat. When it is hot, add the garlic and sauté just until barely golden, about 1 minute. Add the red pepper flakes, olives, anchovies, and oregano or thyme and stir well. Add the tomatoes and cook, uncovered, until slightly thickened, about 5 minutes. Stir in the parsley, capers, and pepper. Taste for salt, adding a little if needed.

2 Use the sauce hot with pasta, or serve it at room temperature with fish or vegetables.

Salty anchovies, in one form or another, often accompany an aperitif, working together to open up the appetite. This is a rather sophisticated rendition but nearly effortless to make. Pass the puffs on a tray, or set them out in baskets.

ANCHOVY PUFFS   makes 120 puffs; serves about 20

$^1/_4$ cup extra-virgin olive oil

6 cloves garlic, coarsely chopped

4 ounces anchovy fillets, cut into $^1/_2$-inch pieces

1 sheet puff pastry, about 10 by 12 inches and $^1/_4$ inch
   thick, thawed if frozen

$^1/_4$ cup minced fresh thyme

1 Preheat an oven to 350°F. Line a baking sheet with parchment paper.

2 Combine the olive oil and garlic in a mortar, small food processor, or blender. Addthe anchovy fillets. Crush with a pestle or process to make a thin paste, but do not purée. There should be bits of anchovy.

3 On a lightly floured work surface, lay out the puff pastry sheet. Using a floured rolling pin, roll it out just enough to smooth any creases. Transfer the pastry to the baking sheet and brush the surface evenly with the anchovy paste. Using a pizza cutter or a sharp knife, cut the pastry into 1-inch squares. Top each square with a pinch of thyme.

4 Bake until the tops have turned golden brown and the pastry has risen almost 1 inch high, 25 to 30 minutes. Serve hot or at room temperature.

olives, anchovies, and capers

Here is a savory pastry that combines a traditional pastry from northern Europe with a lusty Mediterranean filling.

BLACK OLIVE and ANCHOVY STRUDEL serves 8

1 teaspoon unsalted butter (optional)

1^1/$_2$ cups (about ^{1}/$_2$ pound) oil-cured black olives, pitted and coarsely chopped

2 ounces olive oil–packed sun-dried tomatoes, drained and chopped

12 anchovy fillets, chopped

1 teaspoon minced fresh thyme

^{1}/$_2$ teaspoon freshly ground black pepper

1 to 2 tablespoons extra-virgin olive oil

1 sheet puff pastry, about 14 by 15 inches and ^{1}/$_4$ inch thick, thawed

1 egg yolk beaten with 1 tablespoon water

1 Preheat an oven to 375°F. Line a baking sheet with parchment paper or grease it with the butter.

2 In a bowl, combine the olives, tomatoes, anchovies, thyme, pepper, and 1 tablespoon olive oil. Mix well and add more olive oil as needed to create a spreadable mixture.

3 On a lightly floured work surface, lay out the puff pastry sheet. Using a floured rolling pin, roll it out just enough to smooth any creases. Transfer the pastry to the prepared baking sheet.

4 Spread the filling lengthwise on one-half of the pastry sheet, coming to within about ^{1}/$_2$ inch of the edge. Using a pastry brush, spread some of the egg yolk mixture along the edges. Fold the uncovered half of the pastry over the filling and press the edges together to seal. Using a sharp knife, cut 3-inch-long diagonal slits about 2 inches apart into the top of the pastry. Gently brush with the remaining egg yolk mixture, again being careful not to drip over the edges.

5 Place in the oven and bake until the pastry is puffed and golden brown, 20 to 25 minutes. Remove and let stand for at least 5 minutes. To serve, cut into slices or squares. Serve hot or at room temperature.

Pan bagnat is a famous salad sandwich of the French Riviera filled with tuna, tomatoes, and eggs, then seasoned with anchovies, olives, and capers. In this spicy version, the rolls are sprinkled with a little chile pepper as well as olive oil and vinegar, although in France, *harissa*, the North African hot sauce of red chiles, garlic, and caraway or cumin, would be used.

SPICY PAN BAGNAT makes 4 sandwiches

4 large, round chewy rolls

$1/_3$ cup extra-virgin olive oil

2 tablespoons red wine vinegar

2 teaspoons chile powder such as New Mexican,
  preferably freshly ground

4 ounces olive oil–packed tuna

2 tomatoes, thinly sliced

2 hard-boiled eggs, peeled and thinly sliced

12 anchovy fillets

2 tablespoons capers, rinsed and drained

$1/_4$ cup pitted salt-cured black olives

4 to 8 lettuces leaves such as red leaf, green leaf, or butterhead

Cut the rolls in half horizontally and sprinkle the cut sides evenly with the olive oil, vinegar, and chile powder. Drain and flake the tuna, then divide it evenly among the bottom halves of the rolls. Compose the sandwiches by evenly dividing the tomatoes, eggs, anchovies, capers, olives, and lettuce leaves among them. Cover with the roll tops and serve.

Anchovies and olives are often added to breads and savory pastries in the southern swaths of both Italy and France. Adding a little anchovy topping to focaccia gives the flat bread a pizza-like quality. When cut into wedges or squares, it can be eaten on its own as an appetizer or snack, or it can be served along with an antipasto platter.

ANCHOVY FOCACCIA   makes one 10-inch-by-12-inch sheet; serves 8

For the dough:
2 packages (2^1/$_2$ teaspoons each) active dry yeast
1^1/$_2$ cups lukewarm water (108°F)
4^1/$_2$ cups all-purpose flour
^{1}/$_2$ cup plus 2 tablespoons extra-virgin olive oil
1 teaspoon salt
1 tablespoon plus 2 teaspoons minced fresh rosemary

For the topping:
12 to 16 anchovy fillets
^{1}/$_2$ teaspoon salt
1 teaspoon minced fresh rosemary
1 teaspoon freshly ground black pepper
2 tablespoons extra-virgin olive oil

1 To make the dough, in a large bowl, sprinkle the yeast over ^{1}/$_2$ cup of the lukewarm water. Let stand until foamy, about 5 minutes. Add 4 cups of the flour, the remaining 1 cup warm water, ^{1}/$_4$ cup of the olive oil, the salt, and the rosemary. Mix with a wooden spoon and then with floured hands until a soft, sticky dough forms. Cover the bowl with a damp kitchen towel, place it in a warm spot, and let the dough rise until not quite doubled in size, about 1^1/$_2$ hours.

2 Punch down the dough and then remove it from the bowl. Form the dough into a loose ball. Using ^{1}/$_4$ cup of the olive oil, coat the inside of a clean bowl. Place the ball of dough in the bowl and turn the dough to coat it evenly with the oil. Cover the bowl with a damp kitchen towel and let rise again in a warm spot until nearly doubled in size, 20 to 30 minutes.

3 Preheat an oven to 400°F. Using the remaining 2 tablespoons olive oil, coat the bottom and sides of a 12-by-18-inch (or similar-sized) baking sheet.

4 Dust a work surface with the remaining ½ cup flour. Turn out the dough onto the floured surface, punch it down, and then flatten it out by stretching it with your hands equally from all sides. It should be about 10 by 12 inches and ½ inch thick. Carefully transfer the dough to the prepared baking sheet–it will be smaller than the baking sheet–and dimple the dough with your fingertips or the end of a handle of a wooden spoon, making small indentations where the olive oil can pool. Space the dimples evenly and make them about ½ inch deep.

5 To top the focaccia, distribute the anchovies evenly over the surface and sprinkle all over with the salt, rosemary, and pepper. Baste the top with the olive oil.

6 Bake the focaccia until golden brown, 20 to 25 minutes. Transfer to a rack and let cool for at least 5 minutes. Serve hot, warm, or at room temperature, cut into squares, wedges, or thin slices.

spreads, sauces, and breads

La *reine* is one of the great pizzas of Provence, an intensely flavored combination of anchovies, olives, and capers, plus goat cheese. It is sold ready-made at the pizza wagons or temporary stalls that seem to be at every open market and is served at restaurants as well. When I make it at home, I like to add an extra dollop or two of cheese, which is reflected in the recipe below. If your food processor lacks the capacity or the power to mix the dough, it is easily mixed and kneaded by hand or in a stand mixer.

LA REINE PIZZA   makes four 6-inch pizzas, or two 12-inch pizzas; serves 4

For the crust:

2 envelopes (2$^{1}/_{2}$ teaspoons each) active dry yeast

1 cup lukewarm water (108°F)

1 teaspoon sugar

1 teaspoon salt

2 tablespoons extra-virgin olive oil

about 3$^{1}/_{2}$ cups all-purpose flour

Cornmeal for dusting pans

For the topping:

$^{1}/_{4}$ cup extra-virgin olive oil

$^{1}/_{2}$ cup freshly made tomato sauce

12 anchovy fillets

2 teaspoons capers, rinsed and drained

$^{1}/_{4}$ cup salt-cured black olives

6 ounces fresh goat cheese

2 tablespoons minced fresh thyme

$^{1}/_{4}$ cup grated Parmesan cheese

$^{1}/_{4}$ cup chopped fresh marjoram

1 To make the dough, in a small bowl, dissolve the yeast in the lukewarm water. Add the sugar and let stand until foamy, about 5 minutes.

continued

spreads, sauces, and breads

2 In a food processor, combine the yeast mixture, salt, 1 table-spoon of the olive oil, and 3 cups of the flour. Process until the ingredients come together into a ball. If the dough is too wet, add more flour, a little at a time, until a smooth, firm-textured ball forms. If the dough is too dry, add dribbles of warm water until the ball forms. Continue to process until the dough is silky but firm, 3 to 4 minutes longer. Turn the dough out onto a well-floured board and knead until smooth and elastic, 4 to 5 minutes.

3 Using the remaining 1 tablespoon olive oil, oil a large bowl. Place the dough in the bowl and turn the ball to coat its surface with oil. Cover the bowl with a clean cloth and let stand in a warm place until the dough has doubled in size, 1 to 1$\frac{1}{2}$ hours. Punch down the dough in the bowl, cover it again with the cloth, and let it rest for another 30 minutes.

4 Position a rack in the upper third of the oven and preheat the oven to 500°F.

5 Divide the dough into 4 equal portions. On a lightly floured work surface, roll out each portion into a round $\frac{1}{8}$ inch thick and about 6 inches in diameter. Alternatively, divide the dough into 2 portions and roll out to make 2 rounds each 12 inches in diameter. Sprinkle 2 baking sheets or pizza pans with cornmeal and transfer the dough rounds to the pans.

6 To top the pizzas, brush or drizzle the rounds with some of the olive oil, then spread with the tomato sauce. Divide the anchovies, capers, and olives evenly among the rounds. Dot with the goat cheese, and sprinkle with the thyme and Parmesan cheese. Slip a baking sheet or pizza pan onto the upper rack of the oven and bake until the bottom of the crust(s) is crisp and the edges are lightly browned, 10 to 12 minutes. Remove from the oven, and immediately slip the remaining pizza pan or baking sheet onto the rack. Drizzle the baked pizza(s) with half the remaining olive oil, then sprinkle with half of the marjoram. Repeat with the remaining pizza(s). Serve at once.

Anchovies and tomatoes give this tart's cheese custard filling a Mediterranean air and an earthy, hearty flavor. The toppings sink slightly into the filling as it bakes, producing a lovely unpretentious presentation at the table.

FRESH TOMATO TART with ANCHOVIES

serves 6

For the crust:

2 cups all-purpose flour

$^1/_2$ teaspoon salt

$^1/_2$ cup chilled unsalted butter

6 tablespoons ice water

For the filling:

3 eggs

1 cup heavy cream

1 cup half-and-half

$^1/_2$ teaspoon freshly ground black pepper

3 tomatoes, cut into generous $^1/_2$-inch-thick slices

8 to 10 anchovy fillets

1 teaspoon fresh thyme, minced

2 tablespoons grated Parmesan cheese

2 tablespoons grated or slivered Gruyère cheese

1 To make the crust, in a bowl, combine the flour and salt and mix well. Cut the butter into $^1/_2$-inch chunks and add them to the flour mixture. Using a pastry blender or 2 knives, cut the butter into the flour until pea-sized balls form. Add the ice water, 1 tablespoon at a time. As you add the water, turn the mixture lightly with a fork and then with your fingertips to keep the pastry light and flaky. It will cling together in a rough mass. Gather the dough into a ball–it will be a little crumbly–wrap it in plastic wrap, and refrigerate for 15 minutes. Meanwhile, preheat an oven to 425°F.

continued

spreads, sauces, and breads

2 On a lightly floured work surface, roll out the dough into a round ¼ inch thick. Carefully transfer to a straight-sided 9-inch tart pan with 1-inch sides. Line the pastry with aluminum foil or parchment paper and add pastry weights or dried beans.

3 Bake until set, 12 to 15 minutes. Remove from the oven and remove the weights and foil or parchment. Prick any bubbles with the tines of a fork and return to the oven until firm and bisque-colored, about 5 minutes longer. Remove from the oven, place on a baking sheet, and let cool before filling. Reduce the oven to 375°F.

4 To make the filling, in a bowl, combine the eggs, cream, half-and-half, and pepper and mix well. Pour the egg mixture into the partially baked pastry crust. Top with the sliced tomatoes, then arrange the anchovies, pinwheel fashion, on top. Sprinkle evenly with the thyme and the Parmesan and Gruyère cheeses.

5 Carefully transfer the baking sheet to the oven and bake the tart until the top is puffed and lightly golden and a knife inserted into the center comes out clean, 25 to 30 minutes. Transfer to a rack and let stand for at least 15 minutes before cutting. Serve hot or at room temperature.

Savory little bread dishes are both snack food and appetizers in the Mediterranean. You can find them as tapas in Spain, mezze in Greece, and as quick bites in street stalls in Provence, Sicily, and sunny Tunisia.

MEDITERRANEAN GALETTES serves 4

1 large or 2 medium red sweet peppers
1 teaspoon unsalted butter (optional)
1 sheet puff pastry, about 14 by 15 inches and $1/4$ inch thick, thawed if frozen
$1/4$ cup milk, half-and-half, or heavy cream
4 ounces fresh goat cheese
2 tablespoons extra-virgin olive oil
1 clove garlic, minced
$1/2$ teaspoon salt
$1/4$ cup salt-cured black olives
6 anchovy fillets, minced
1 tablespoon minced fresh flat-leaf parsley
$1/2$ teaspoon freshly ground black pepper

1 Preheat a broiler. Place the sweet pepper(s) on a broiler tray and slide under the broiler. Broil, turning as necessary to color evenly, until blackened on all sides. Slip the pepper(s) into a plastic bag and close the top. Let stand to allow the skins to steam and loosen, 4 to 5 minutes. Remove the pepper(s) from the bag and peel off the blackened skin. Pull out or cut along the stem(s), slit lengthwise, and remove the seeds and ribs. Chop coarsely and set aside.

2 Preheat an oven to 375°F. Line a baking sheet with parchment paper or grease it with the butter.

3 On a lightly floured work surface, lay out the puff pastry sheet. Using a floured rolling pin, roll it out just enough to smooth any creases. Using a cookie cutter, jar lid, or widemouthed glass 4 to 5 inches in diameter, cut out 4 rounds.

4 Place the rounds on the prepared baking sheet about 2 inches apart In a small bowl, blend the milk with the goat cheese. Divide the cheese mixture evenly among the rounds, placing it so that when it melts it will spread out to, but not over, the edges. In a bowl, combine the chopped roasted pepper, olive oil, garlic, and salt, and turn them to mix thoroughly. Put the pepper mixture on the goat cheese, then add the olives, dividing them evenly among the 4 rounds. Sprinkle evenly with the anchovies, parsley, and black pepper. Using your fingertips, push against the edges of the pastry, crimping it inward slightly.

5 Bake the *galettes* until puffed and golden, about 20 minutes. Remove from the oven and let rest for 5 minutes before serving. Serve hot or warm.

All of these businesses have mail-order catalogs that, in addition to offering capers, anchovies, and olives, carry many high-quality Mediterranean pantry items, including a wide variety of extra-virgin olive oils and of vinegars.

ZINGERMAN'S DELICATESSEN

Ann Arbor, MI

Tel: 313-663-3400

Olives, salted capers, salt- and olive oil–packed anchovies.

DEAN & DELUCA

New York, NY

Tel: 800-221-7714

Olives, salted capers, salt- and olive oil–packed anchovies.

VIVANDE

San Francisco, CA

Tel: 415-346-4430

Olives, salted capers from Pantelleria, salt- and olive oil–packed anchovies.

MANICARETTI

Oakland, CA

Tel: 800-799-9830

Olives, salted capers from Pantelleria and Salina, salt- and olive oil–packed anchovies, tapenades.

olives, anchovies, and capers

ACKNOWLEDGMENTS

Thank you to my faithful testers and eaters, Ethel, Laurent, Oliver, Dan, Tom, and Jim, and a special thank you to Candice Kimberling for helping with recipe testing. Thank you to the people at Oldways, Foodcom, and The International Olive Oil Council for making research trips possible. Thank you to the many, many people whose ideas, suggestions, knowledge, and comments helped me arrive at what I have included in this book, among them Faith Heller Willinger, Anna Tosca Lanza, Dana Jacobi, Nancy Harmon Jenkins, Charlotte Kimball, Peggy Knickerbocker, Joyce Goldstein, Seen Lippert, Fred Plotkin, Debra Krasner, and Paula Wolfert. A special thank you to my agent, Susan Lescher, and to Bill LeBlond, my editor at Chronicle Books. As always, deep gratitude and appreciation to my husband, Jim, for all his help and support throughout the days and years on this project and so many others. Thank you especially to Sharon Silva, with whom I have had the privilege to work on many of my Chronicle Books. Like a good therapist, she asks the questions that let you discover the way.

olives, anchovies, and capers

olives, anchovies, and capers

The exact equivalents in the following tables have been rounded for convenience.

LIQUID/DRY MEASURES

U.S.	METRIC
1/4 teaspoon	1.25 milliliters
1/2 teaspoon	2.5 milliliters
1 teaspoon	5 milliliters
1 tablespoon (3 teaspoons)	15 milliliters
1 fluid ounce (2 tablespoons)	30 milliliters
1/4 cup	60 milliliters
1/3 cup	80 milliliters
1/2 cup	120 milliliters
1 cup	240 milliliters
1 pint (2 cups)	480 milliliters
1 quart (4 cups, 32 ounces)	960 milliliters
1 gallon (4 quarts)	3.84 liters
1 ounce (by weight)	28 grams
1 pound	454 grams
2.2 pounds	1 kilogram

OVEN TEMPERATURE

FAHRENHEIT	CELSIUS	GAS
250	120	1/2
275	140	1
300	150	2
325	160	3
350	180	4
375	190	5
400	200	6
425	220	7
450	230	8
475	240	9
500	260	10

LENGTH

U.S.	METRIC
1/8 inch	3 millimeters
1/4 inch	6 millimeters
1/2 inch	12 millimeters
1 inch	2.5 centimeters

olives, anchovies, and capers

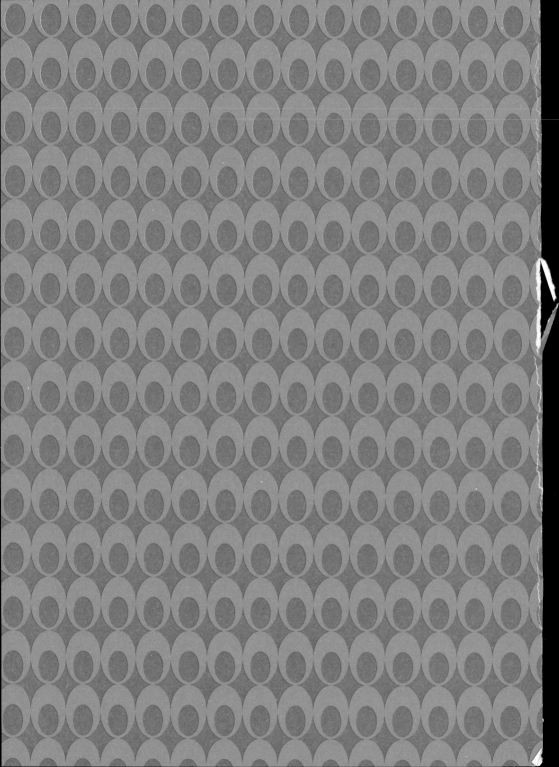